HIS
MYSTERIOUS
WAYS

His Mysterious Ways

More than Coincidence

edited by EVELYN BENCE

foreword by EDWARD GRINNAN

His Mysterious Ways
Published by Guideposts
16 East 34th Street
New York, New York 10016
www.guideposts.com

ACKNOWLEDGMENTS
Every attempt has been made to credit the sources of copyrighted
material used in this book. If any such acknowledgment has been
inadvertently omitted or miscredited, receipt of such information
would be appreciated.

Scripture quotations are taken from *The Holy Bible, New King
James Version*. Copyright © 1997, 1990, 1985, 1983 by Thomas
Nelson, Inc.

Cover design by Kathleen Lynch
Cover image by Getty Images
Interior design by Gretchen Schuler-Dandridge
Typeset by Aptara

Printed and bound in the United States of America
10 9 8 7 6 5 4 3 2 1

Contents

His Mysterious Ways

FOREWORD

One night I was trying to explain to a group of non-*Guideposts* magazine readers (yes, such people exist) what a "His Mysterious Ways" story was and why the feature was so beloved by our subscribers. "Oh," said a man finally, "it's like that old TV show *Unsolved Mysteries*." The others nodded, seeming to agree that he had hit the nail on the head. "Not quite," I was forced to say, "because there's no mystery about 'Mysterious Ways.'"

No mystery? They looked at me as if I were talking nonsense. Then why on earth call it "His Mysterious Ways"?

Why, indeed.

One of the first "Mysterious Ways" I read when I got to Guideposts was about a young mother whose son was inside a kindergarten classroom when a tornado struck the building. Out of her mind with worry, she called the school and was reassured by someone answering the phone that all of the children were safe. "Your son is all right," the kind voice said. School officials would be in touch. The mother hung up, immensely relieved and grateful. Hours later, the school finally called to tell her that her son was unharmed and where she could pick him up. The officials were baffled, however, when the mother mentioned the first call. The building had been completely evacuated well before the tornado hit and, besides, the phone service had been knocked out for hours. No one could have possibly answered. Then who was the person on the other end of the line with those comforting words, "Your son is all right"?

New to Guideposts and coming from a journalistic background, I was suspicious. Surely there was a logical explanation for all of this. I took it upon myself to investigate, combing through the story file and double-checking the facts. I was frustrated I could find nothing to justify my skepticism. The mother was completely believable, and the school confirmed the particulars of the incident. No one could have answered the phone.

Still, during that first year or so at Guideposts, I persisted in playing the role of gadfly, always trying to find a rational explanation for every "Mysterious Ways" that dropped over the transom. At one of our weekly editorial meetings, Van Varner, then the editor-in-chief, threw up his hands and shouted at me, "If YOU were in charge of 'His Mysterious Ways,' we would never have any!"

Wouldn't you know it? I *am* in charge of "His Mysterious Ways," and we have plenty, as the book you are about to read attests. Story after story offering hope, reassurance, comfort and guidance. Wondrous accounts of unspoken prayers answered, unknown yearnings realized, unexpected healings received. Each and every one true.

Have I grown less skeptical through the years? Actually, no. We still choose these stories very carefully and check them out thoroughly. But my understanding of what lies at the heart of this unique feature's overwhelming popularity has closely paralleled my spiritual growth, as I've been able to see a divine hand at work in my life in ways that never cease to astonish and inspire me.

God's ways may be mysterious, but His presence and purposes are not. Which is why "Mysterious Ways" are never unsolved mysteries.

Edward Grinnan
Editor-in-Chief, *Guideposts*

INTRODUCTION

God moves in a mysterious way
His wonders to perform;
He plants his footsteps in the sea,
And rides upon the storm.

Ye fearful saints, fresh courage take;
The clouds you so much dread
Are big with mercy, and shall break
In blessings on your head.

William Cowper (1731–1800)

As children and teens, my siblings and I would gather around the piano late on Sunday afternoons to sing through the hymnbook. That's where I grew to appreciate this hymn by the British poet William Cowper. Years later I learned more about Mr. Cowper, who was befriended by his neighbor and pastor, John Newton (author of "Amazing Grace"). Mr. Cowper wrote these lines based on his personal experience of faith amid—or despite—professional failure, overwhelming anxiety and deep depression that prompted several mysteriously thwarted suicide attempts. Sensing the hymn's power,

Pastor Newton published it, and indeed its message is as true today as it was two hundred years ago.

"God moves in a mysterious way." It's an underlying theme of every personal story in this newly compiled book, Guideposts' fifth volume of *His Mysterious Ways*. In keeping with the format of the popular "His Mysterious Ways" column of *Guideposts* magazine, most of the selected stories are very short, giving just the highlights of an unusual encounter with a stranger, a perfectly timed provision, an unexpected reconnection with a "lost" person or possession, a prayer answered by a surprising turn of events. A few of the true stories in each section are longer, fleshing out the details of God's dramatic work; one of my favorites is "Heaven's Trail," in which God miraculously honors a woman's memory of her recently deceased father.

Turn the page. Again and again you'll find reason to take "fresh courage," bolstered by a new awareness of God's watchful presence and inexplicable ways. The mystery starts with a phone call unaccountably routed to Anaheim, California.

—*Evelyn Bence*

· 1 ·

GIVING ASSURANCE

"I AM WITH YOU ALWAYS,
EVEN TO THE END OF THE AGE."
—*Matthew 28:20*

*Lord, remind us today that we are not
traveling alone on this life journey.*

CROSSING THE LINES

Terri Kilroy

Ten o'clock and I'm still at the office, I thought. I'd been putting in a lot of extra hours lately. I barely had a moment to think, pray, talk to my friends—just to relax. Everyone else had left hours ago. I'd promised myself I would get home early tonight. So why was I still at work? *Just one more fax,* I told myself. *Then I'll leave.*

I put the papers on the machine and punched in the number of a client in Los Angeles. Then I pressed the "send" button. An error message flashed on the display beside the number. I looked at it closely. *Odd. That's not the number I dialed.* This one was a 714 area code. *That's Anaheim,* I thought. *Why would the fax machine be calling there?* I tried again, carefully dialing my client's number. The same thing happened.

Finally, I decided to call the mysterious 714 number. The phone rang a few times. Then a woman answered shakily, "Hello?"

I explained to her that I had been trying to send a fax.

"There's no fax machine here," she said. "This is a convalescent home. You called an old lady."

I quickly apologized for bothering her so late at night.

"Oh no, my dear, I'm glad you called. I hardly ever get any visitors. In fact, I was just sitting here asking the Lord for a friendly voice."

The old woman and I chatted for a few minutes. Then a few more. She told me all about her life in the nursing home. I talked about my job. Before I knew it, we were talking about faith too.

"Thank you so much for calling, dear," the woman finally said. "You made my night."

Now it was really late. But all the way home a good feeling stayed with me. I didn't even think about the fax until the next day, when I got to work. I called my client to apologize for not sending him the papers.

"What do you mean?" he asked. "I got your fax late last night. It came in just after ten."

I guess I must have had the right number all along.

"MIJO, THE LORD WILL PROVIDE"

Isaac J. Canales

It was the one day of the year Mama didn't put beans and tortillas or even her specialty—tamales—on the table. When it came to celebrating Thanksgiving, we were as American as anybody else. Cranberry sauce, pumpkin and mincemeat pies, turkey, mashed potatoes and gravy—all that and stuffing too. Mama made the best.

But the year I was eleven, we hadn't even begun our holiday preparations by the time the end of November rolled around. And I knew why.

Papa and Mama were pastors of a little church in Keystone (now Carson), California. We were poor—so poor our rent in the projects, twenty-six dollars a month, was almost more than we could handle. We lived on whatever the congregation could afford to give. That fall, times were hard for everyone, and offerings hit an all-time low. I watched the tambourine we used for a collection plate very, very closely.

Nervously I asked Mama about our Thanksgiving dinner. "Isaac, God will provide," she replied. "You know he has always been faithful to us." I remembered the shoes, winter coats, even parts for the family car that had arrived just when we needed them. Maybe Mama was right. But time was running out. I waited anxiously for something to happen.

Soon the holiday was upon us. I could hear the tambourine rattle dully as a few meager coins hit the skin. *Why hasn't God stepped in?* I wondered.

I asked Mama again if we would have turkey. "*Mijo,*" she said (meaning "my son"), "the Lord will provide. Has he ever let us down?"

That kept me quiet until Tuesday. Papa and I went to McCoy's Market for groceries to get us through the week—a dozen eggs, tortillas, milk. While he was at the checkout, I hurried to the meat department to look at the "toms," as Mama called them. Wistfully I ran my hand over the plump, frozen birds. It wouldn't be Thanksgiving without a turkey.

Wednesday night we gathered in our church, a gutted two-bedroom house with a sign in black-and-yellow letters that read *Misión Ebenezer Asamblea de Dios.* I watched the regulars assemble: Sister Ayala, with her colorful shawl draped around her shoulders; Brother Garcia, who worked in the orchards; and Sister Audrey, a six-foot two-inch seventy-two-year-old former B-movie extra who played the violin and wore a dark fur coat. My family and a few others made up the rest of the congregation that evening.

I tugged on Mama's sleeve as she headed up to the little blue pump organ next to the pulpit. "I know there won't be enough for Thanksgiving dinner," I said. "What are we going to do?"

"Shh," she whispered, looking serene as always. "Don't worry, *mijo*, the Lord will provide." If that were true, wouldn't he have done something by now?

The service began. Mama played the organ, Papa strummed the guitar and Sister Audrey joined in on her violin as we sang "There Is Power in the Blood" in Spanish. Papa spoke about the holiday being a time to give thanks to the Lord for his provision. Then he called me: "Isaac, would you please pick up the tithes and offerings tonight? And would you ask the Lord to bless them?"

It was an honor to be asked to participate in the service, but it was the last thing I wanted that night. I mumbled a prayer for the few coins I knew were all that would be forthcoming. After I said amen and raised my head, my eyes caught the glitter of a shiny black car pulling up in front of the church. It was the longest and newest car I had ever seen. The door opened and a tall, handsome man dressed in a tuxedo stepped out. He looked like Clark Gable, right down to his pencil-thin mustache. He came in and sat in the second pew. I could tell by the puzzled glances that the whole congregation wondered who he was.

I'm sure Mama played offertory music that night, but all I could hear was the thud of the coins as they dropped into the tambourine. I slowly worked my way around the room toward the elegant stranger until finally I stood directly in front of him.

A hint of a smile played around his lips. He reached into his jacket pocket, pulled out a cloth napkin and slipped it onto the tambourine. It was so heavy that I had to steady the tambourine with both hands. "Thank you!" I croaked as I watched twenty silver dollars roll out of the napkin.

Returning to the front of the church, I could not contain my happiness. Mama was staring at me curiously. I pointed to the tambourine and mouthed *turkey*. She didn't look surprised; she just smiled and launched into a rousing rendition of "When the Saints Go Marching In."

The stranger slipped out before the service ended, before anyone could ask who had sent him. I didn't have to ask. I knew. The next evening, as Papa asked the blessing for our Thanksgiving feast, I silently added a prayer of my own: *Thank you, God, for always being faithful. From now on I'll try to be too.* Mama's turkey and dressing had never tasted better.

Mama is in heaven now. I am the pastor of Papa's church. We have grown to more than one thousand members and have a beautiful new church building only three blocks from that two-bedroom house. I still sometimes worry about how our needs will be met, especially since my wife and I have three teenage sons. Then I hear Mama's whisper in my ear, "Don't worry, *mijo*. The Lord will provide." And he does. Not always as dramatically as that long-ago Thanksgiving eve, but just as surely.

$\mathcal{A}$ SURE SIGN

Jeff Kuwik

$\mathcal{M}$om grew up with two deaf parents. A lot of people might be frustrated by that situation, but Mom embraced it. She devoted her life to helping the deaf as a sign-language interpreter. From the time we were little, my sister and I picked up all the signs, especially the one for "I love you"—the two middle fingers bent inward, the index finger, pinkie and thumb extended. That's how we always said good-bye.

When she was in her forties, Mom got sick. Cancer. Even so, she cared more about me and my sister than she did about herself, always making sure we were okay. "Don't worry about me; focus on your work," she said about my job at Buffalo Wireworks, making screens and cutting sheet metal. *Were they treating me well?* she wanted to know. *Did my work gloves protect my hands?* Mom grew weaker. After a year-long battle, she died.

It was two weeks before I could drag myself back into work. Walking into the metal shop that first day, I tried hard to focus. But I just missed Mom so much. I walked over to my station to grab my gloves and goggles and get ready for the day.

The first thing I noticed were my gloves, on the table, not usually where I left them, lying neatly side by side, as if someone had put them there. *That's strange,* I thought. Then I noticed something startling. The right glove was crumpled a bit. The two middle fingers were bent inward, the index finger, pinkie and thumb extended. The sign for "I love you."

Mom's way of telling me things would be okay.

SOUL SISTERS

Jana Sollars Ketchel

My younger sister, Jennifer, and I were born only thirteen months apart. We shared everything growing up—clothes, toys, friends. We got married and moved into our own houses, but that didn't keep our connection from growing even stronger. Our daughters were born two days apart. Jennifer is the first person I call whenever I need help. And she knows that she can always count on me.

One day last July, Jennifer and I were at our aunt's house for a birthday party. No one noticed Jennifer's two-year-old, Reagan, playing dangerously close to the swimming pool. Not until it was too late.

We pulled Reagan out and laid her beside the pool. She wasn't breathing. Jennifer rushed to her daughter's side. A neighbor performed CPR. "She's going to be okay," I reassured my sister.

Sirens blared and the paramedics rushed in. Jennifer climbed into the back of the ambulance. Without asking, I climbed into the front beside the paramedic. He took one look at my face and decided not to argue.

The whole ride to the hospital, I watched Jennifer through the little window in the ambulance cab. Reagan had an oxygen mask on and a paramedic was leaning over her. My sister looked so scared. *Lord, I wish I could be back there with her.*

Reagan spent seven days in the hospital. By the time she was released, she had completely recovered.

A few weeks later I drove to my sister's house to see Reagan. "I've never been so scared," I told Jennifer as I held Reagan in my lap.

"Me either," Jennifer said. "The ambulance ride was the worst part. Thank God you were there to hold my hand."

"What do you mean?" I asked. "I was sitting up front with the driver."

Jennifer gave me a puzzled look. "No, Jana. You were right next to me. You kept patting my knee and telling me that everything would be okay."

My sister and I stared at each other—speechless. I guess we're even closer than we knew.

THE VISITOR AT THE WAKE

Yvonne Luttrell

*J*ust days before, my only daughter, Nichole, was a senior in high school, her whole life ahead of her. Now I was standing beside her coffin, asking God how I could go on after a car accident had taken her from me forever. So many people had come to offer condolences, but I couldn't bring myself to speak to them. These were my last moments with Nichole. I refused to leave her. My father stood beside me, greeting people so I wouldn't have to.

An older man in a cream-colored suit greeted me with a hug. Why wasn't Dad stepping in? As soon as the man released me, I turned back to Nichole. "See how beautiful she is?" the man said. "That's the way she will look when you see her again."

Again? I wanted to ask, but just then a soft, white light appeared around Nichole. It seemed to hold her in a powerful embrace that was not of this world. For the first time since the accident, I thought about something other than my grief. I thought about Nichole. *Now she knows ever-lasting peace,* it struck me as the light faded away.

I spun around to ask the man if he'd seen the light too. I scanned the room for his cream suit, but everyone was dressed in dark colors.

"Who was that man just talking to me?" I asked Dad.

"I haven't let anyone disturb you, Yvonne. Let's sit down for a while."

"Thanks, Dad," I said, knowing the next time I saw Nichole it would be forever.

MESSENGERS IN THE NIGHT

Betsi Fox

I threw my duffel bag of clothes, a couple of cans of soda and my rifle onto the bottom of the skiff and dragged it into the water. Bruiser, our ninety-pound German shepherd, scrambled into the bow as I checked the gas and made sure the extra tank was full.

For just a moment I hesitated. I'd never taken a boat this small into the choppy open water off the Alaska coast. The skiff was a twelve-foot fiberglass affair with an outboard motor that buzzed like a sick bee. The boat didn't even have oars, just an old snow shovel to paddle with in a pinch. But shucks, I'd lived alone in the bush, caught my own food, faced down grizzly bears—how hard could a little boat trip be?

I did a balancing act as I tugged at the starter cord. The engine was old and temperamental, but it finally caught and off we puttered. My four-year-old daughter, Becca, and the other kids at our makeshift school waved good-bye from the shore as I rounded the point. Off by myself at last! It was a sunny July day in 1979, the sea calm after three weeks of nonstop wind and rain. I leaned back against my duffel, drinking in the solitude and the sunlight as we crept past a chain of uninhabited spruce-clad islands, Bruiser barking at every drifting log and floating otter.

I didn't know how long going back to our home island would take. Becca and I had always come here in my husband's big fishing trawler—just over a two-hour trip with the powerful diesel engine. He'd brought the skiff along so I could poke around in the sheltered cove of the island where the school was located. Many fishermen's families lived, as we did, on isolated islands, and we solved the problem of school by bringing our children together on the island with the largest cabin. Mothers took turns teaching, three or four days at a stretch. But no sooner had my latest stint begun than stormy weather set in, marooning me for three weeks, the only adult with fifteen cooped-up kids. When the weather finally broke and my replacement arrived, I was ready to take off for home on anything that floated.

Now we were making slower progress than I'd reckoned on. We'd gone barely a third of the way when the motor gave an ominous sputter and died.

Out of gas already! I'd have to stop at the small town of Sitka, our local "metropolis," to refuel. I hooked up the spare tank and then pulled the starter cord. Nothing. I tried again. A cough, then silence. I took a break, cracked the top of a soda, shared some with Bruiser and then tackled the outboard again. Rocking the boat in my exertions, I spilled the rest of the can. When at last the engine turned over, I celebrated with my second and last pop, again sharing it with Bruiser.

Four hours later it was getting dark and I was starting to worry. I should have sighted Sitka by now! Had I taken a wrong turn among the maze of islands? The temperature was dropping fast, the frigid Alaska night coming on. I pulled a jacket from my duffel bag and wondered how much gas was left. So typical of me—in a rush to go off by myself, all my life preferring unknown dangers ahead to what lay behind.

It had started in my childhood with my stepmother and the harsh, judgmental God she'd held over me. A rigid, sanctimonious woman, she showed a pious face to the world and saved her violent rages for me. Ten years earlier, on my nineteenth birthday, I'd put a knapsack and a sleeping bag on my back and hitchhiked as far as I could go from Ohio, fearing every mile that the angry policeman of a God she'd preached at me was hot on my heels.

It took me thirteen days to thumb five thousand miles. I ended up in Alaska and have made it my home ever since, marrying and raising a family on a remote island twelve miles from the nearest neighbor.

I was accustomed to roughing it, but this boat trip had become more than I bargained for. I was cold, thirsty and ravenously hungry by the time I saw the lights of Sitka in the distance. I groaned with relief. Moments later I heard an all-too-familiar sputter. The engine coughed twice and went dead. The last gas was gone—and I was still miles from town.

Keep calm, I told myself. *You've managed alone before.*

If I could make it to land, any land, I'd simply build a fire and wait for morning, when I could signal a passing fishing boat. I grabbed the shovel and stroked as hard as I could in the direction of the nearest island. Its shadowy outline only got farther away. The tide was going out! The current was too strong to row against, even if I'd had oars.

Bruiser! My big dog was a powerful swimmer. If I tied the bow-rope around his neck, would he be able to tow the boat to shore? I secured the rope around him all right, but when I tried to push him from the boat, he gave a low whine that said all too clearly, "No way am I going in that freezing water."

There was nothing to do but watch the lights of Sitka grow dimmer as the slap of the waves carried us into the open sea. I dug out every warm thing I had in the duffel bag and hunkered down. Surely in the morning a fishing boat would see us!

I did see boats the next day, but they were far in the distance—wooden specks on the vast blue ocean. I tied my red bathrobe to the end of the shovel and waved it and shouted till I had no voice left.

There were two bullets in my rifle. Desperate, I fired them both, knowing even as I did that the noise of the boats' engines would most likely drown out the sound.

Farther and farther from land we drifted. The sun beat down on the open skiff, cracking my lips, cheeks, forehead. I knew better than to drink seawater, but that afternoon I got so hot that I splashed some on my face. It only blistered the cracked skin.

Night came again, then dawn. That third day I saw boats on the horizon, but I had no strength to wave my shovel and no voice with which to call. As the third night at sea came on, I thought, *I'm going to die.* "If I should die before I wake . . ." The words of the prayer my stepmother made me say on my knees each night, standing over me with a switch in case I left any out, came back to me. "I pray the Lord my soul to take."

No! Anything but that! I hadn't prayed at all in ten years, least of all for my soul to go to my stepmother's vindictive God—a God as angry as she was. I'd come to Alaska to escape—gone where neither she nor he could find me. Bruiser and I would die out here by ourselves, and that was that.

I must have fallen asleep on the cramped floor of the skiff because I was awakened by icy water splashing on my face. There was an explosive exhalation, followed by something scraping softly against the side of the boat.

Struggling to sit up straight, I stared out over the moonlit sea.

And then I saw them. Great black-and-white shapes gliding past. Now on the other side, circling round. A pod of orca whales, surrounding and dwarfing my tiny craft. One, two, four, seven—nine of the colossal creatures!

Bruiser, who would ordinarily bark at anything that moved, sat quietly beside me, his head in my lap.

A few yards away one of the giants breached and then dove. The whale's flukes were bigger than the boat, yet they left barely a ripple on the sea's placid surface. The merest flick of that tail would certainly have capsized us.

The whale breached again, spouting water through its blowhole with a great whoosh but again barely rocking the skiff. The next time one of the orcas brushed up against the boat, I reached out to touch its smooth skin. It stayed close, as though it liked to be petted.

All through the night, the pod circled the boat, calling out to each other—and to me too, I imagined—with squeaks and whistles. *What are they saying?* I wondered.

Are they concerned at finding a fellow creature alone? Staying near to keep me company? Adrift at sea, distant as I'd ever managed to be, I was confronted with a nearness I trembled to name.

Who had sent me these giant creatures to give the lie to the word alone? I wondered. The answer was too large, too obvious to miss. How could I have let my stepmother's anger blind me to the truth that breathed in the water all around? God had pursued me—I'd been absolutely right about that. But not to punish me. *Sometimes,* I thought, *when the distance gets too great, God has to send really big ambassadors to bring us back to him.*

Gently rocked by the circling whales, I at last fell asleep. I woke the next morning to Bruiser's barking and the chug-chug-chug of an engine.

A fishing boat was coming toward me. I looked around for the pod of whales. They were gone, but in their place was the assurance that God will pursue us to the ends of the earth and beyond, not to condemn but to surround us with love.

One of a Kind

Nancy Davis-Greaux

That morning at work, I sat staring at the blank page in my typewriter. I'd been keeping myself busy with my secretarial job, tennis lessons, ski trips and the singles-group meetings at church. I had my close friends and family. But I was lonely. *I just want to feel loved,* I said to God. *Is that so much to ask?*

Lunchtime came around, and I was still struggling with my "poor me" thoughts. *Shopping will do the trick,* I thought, heading for my favorite card shop across the street. For some reason the knickknacks and balloons made me feel worse. A display of brightly colored mugs stood before me. I picked one up to get a closer look. On the side was a red heart and the words *I Love You* written over and over in fancy cursive—the very words I needed to hear. I'll have my afternoon tea in it.

Feeling lighter, I went to the cashier to make my purchase. The clerk checked the mug but couldn't find a price sticker. "I need a price check," he called out to the store manager.

"Where did you find this?" the manager asked me.

"Over there with the others."

The manager walked to the shelf full of mugs and looked for another that said *I Love You.* "That seems to be the only one," he said. "And I don't recall ever selling that style. Take it. No charge." I held the mug tight to my chest. God had blessed me with a sign of his love. And he gave it freely.

$\mathcal{P}$LAY IT AGAIN, MIMI

Sue Martin

$\mathcal{M}$usic played on the jukebox as my husband, Scott, and I took a break from supervising our restaurant. "What's wrong?" Scott asked me.

"I was just thinking about Mimi," I said.

My grandmother Mimi and I had been close growing up. All us grandkids went to her house whenever we could. When we left to go home, she always called, "See you later, alligator!"

"After a while, crocodile," we'd call back, giggling. Even after we grew up we still said good-bye the same way. How I wished I'd been able to say good-bye to Mimi one last time, but a bad case of the flu had kept me from her funeral.

"I guess there's no use wishing for another chance," I said.

I felt a warm hand on my shoulder and turned to say, "Hi." There was no one there. "Who passed behind me?"

"No one," said Scott.

Just at that moment I heard a catchy song coming from the jukebox: "See You Later, Alligator!" It hadn't been on our original playlist.

"When did we get that song on the jukebox?" I asked.

Scott seemed puzzled. We went over to check it out. The song wasn't listed anywhere, not on any track or medley in the whole machine.

The serviceman from the jukebox company could not explain it either. But then, he didn't know about Mimi's special good-bye.

A Celebration
of Baptism

Beverly Roth

Instant messages flew back and forth between my daughter's computer and mine as we planned her baby's baptism. Jennifer and I had communicated this way ever since she and her husband, Marc, moved to Alabama.

Marc wants to do the baptism during the Sunday service, Jennifer wrote. Marc was pastor of St. Andrew's Episcopal Church in Birmingham.

Date, christening gown, menu for the open house afterward—all decided in cyberspace. *It's so good to be planning a happy event!* I typed. How our family needed something to celebrate.

And how festive the church looked when my husband and I arrived in Birmingham for the baptism of six-week-old Isaac. *Not like the last time we were here,* I thought. It was eight months since my husband and I had last attended a service at St. Andrew's. That day the church had been dimly lit and somber, as befitted a funeral.

This time the sanctuary was aglow with light and color. Proud grandparents, we were ushered down to the front. How strange to sit in the same spot in the same pew where we'd sat for the funeral of Marc and Jennifer's first baby.

Bishop Robert Miller would perform the baptism today, just as he had little Jacob's. But what a contrast in settings. I saw again the sterile cubicle in the cardiac intensive care unit of University of Alabama at Birmingham Hospital, where three-week-old Jacob had just undergone emergency surgery for a congenital heart defect. Only four of us had been admitted to the CICU. Marc, Jennifer, Bishop Miller and I gathered around the small, tilted bed where tiny Jacob lay in a tangle of tubes and wires hooked to life-support systems. A short form of the service, drops of water trickled three times onto baby Jacob's head "in the name of the Father, and the Son, and the Holy Spirit."

Why had the cubicle suddenly seemed so crowded, jammed, overflowing with onlookers? The attending nurse, the four of us—who or what else had entered to share that space?

Bishop Miller had made the sign of the cross in oil on the little forehead: "Jacob, you are sealed with the Spirit in baptism and marked as Christ's own forever."

Forever! I thought. *No matter what.* And above the whir of the monitors, I thought I heard the corridors of eternity ringing in jubilant celebration.

And indeed, with his baptism Jacob did begin to live a new life. Beyond all medical probability he was released from the hospital and lived to be twenty months old. Jacob was a blessing and a joy to all who came near him.

I was brought back to the present as the organ and church choir burst into the opening anthem. There were Bible readings, a hymn, and then Marc entered the pulpit to preach the sermon. He spoke of that earlier baptism in the hospital, and how with it precious baby Jacob was pulled from "practically beyond the brink, and lived . . . and died . . . and still lives!"

It was then that I began to hear a sound I couldn't identify. Something moving, rushing at us. At first I assumed it was a passing train. But there were no train tracks anywhere nearby.

It was something moving fast, something like faraway voices drawing closer, louder. I wondered if the church's PA system were accidentally picking up some radio signal—at our home church the mike would sometimes broadcast incongruous messages from the police department.

The sound continued and now it was clearly the coming-ever-closer of countless voices, like a throng happily cheering. I was aware suddenly of my own minuteness within something absolutely immense. Was this sound entering our space, or were we entering its space?

Voices, many, many voices became a joyous roar, in no way obliterating Marc's voice from the pulpit, but forming a kind of accompaniment to his story of Jacob's baptism and Isaac's baptism about to come. I wondered if this were the "cloud of witnesses" the Bible speaks of, that throng of watchful ones I'd sensed in the CICU, almost standing on one another's shoulders to crowd into that tiny cubicle where Jacob lay.

Had the witnesses come again? Had they come to see Isaac baptized? Did they attend every baptism?

Or perhaps I was imagining things. Could it be the tinnitus—ringing in the ears—that I'd had for years? But this was completely different. This sound came from far outside me.

I nudged my husband. "What is that incredible noise?" I whispered. He shot me a puzzled look; apparently he was not hearing it at all.

When time came for the baptism, the family marched up the aisle to the marble font near the entrance. Isaac was dressed in the long heirloom gown his great-great-grandmother Mosie had sewn. It was the gown our three girls had worn at their baptisms.

"Isaac," Bishop Miller pronounced, "I baptize you in the name of the Father, and the Son, and the Holy Spirit." Then the words that always choked me up: "Isaac, you are sealed with the Spirit in baptism and marked as Christ's own forever."

Afterward, Marc and Jennifer hosted the open house at their home. I was so busy helping Jennifer with the refreshments I had no time to share my strange experience. With the long drive home that night and returning to work next day, it receded to the back of my mind. Was it possible I'd only dreamed the whole thing?

Ten days later Jennifer and I were instant messaging each other as usual from our computers. *Did I tell you what I heard during the service?* Jennifer wrote. *It started during the sermon—a loud roaring like people at a football game, only louder, and happier. I tried to tune it out, but I kept hearing people shouting, millions of people!*

I stared at the blocks of type popping onto my screen. *Then I saw what looked like a galaxy,* Jennifer's message continued, *only I knew it was actually people, all kind of revolving around a very bright center, and the brightness went through the whole crowd. Of course I thought of Jacob and worried for a second that he could be lost in such a large crowd. But then I saw him up close, happy and shouting and being carried by somebody. It was amazing and beautiful, the whole community of God together and nobody hurting anyone, no one able to be hurt. And I knew that it was a celebration of baptism somehow, a celebration of all baptisms.*

Almost too stunned to make my fingers press the keys, I typed, *I heard it too and wondered what it could be!*

She shot back: *You heard it too?*

For a long time Jennifer and I instant messaged excitedly about the experience we'd unknowingly shared. *It was as if we were being pulled right into heaven,* Jennifer wrote.

Or heaven coming to us, I typed. *I think it will make us see Jacob's death—all death—very differently.* I'd always believed in heaven; it was part of my faith. But never had I imagined the sheer joy and exultation of that realm. Joy magnified a million times for being shared with so many.

I've felt so much joy since Isaac's baptism, Jennifer echoed my thought. *Sad thoughts come, but they're swallowed up in that immense chorus of praise.*

Yes! I typed, and added a row of exclamation points. Death, loss, grief—all sorrow, all questions, swallowed up in the mighty *Hallelujah* we'll all of us sing to God forever.

· 2 ·

KEEPING TRACK

I TRUST IN YOU, O LORD; I SAY, "YOU ARE MY GOD."
MY TIMES ARE IN YOUR HAND. . . .

—*Psalm 31:14–15*

Lord, you keep track of us and what we're doing.
Strategically set us in places where we can
receive—and give—your perfect love.

"DEAR BECKY"

Valarie Ripka

I didn't recognize the return address on the envelope I pulled from the mailbox. *Probably junk mail,* I thought, opening it. To my surprise there were two letters inside. Intrigued, I unfolded one of them. "Dear Val," it began. Dear Val? I had no idea who the letter was from.

"I hope you don't mind that I have located you. Enclosed is a letter, but I had to send an explanation with it. Let me tell you a bit about myself. . . .

"For the past several years, I have endured one struggle after another. The minute I get my head above water, something else pulls me under. Yesterday was one of those times. Going over some papers, I just put my head down and said, 'I cannot do this anymore.'

"The next morning, I went grocery shopping, and in the parking lot, I saw a folded sheet of paper on the ground next to my car. I thought it was someone's grocery list, but something I saw made me pick it up. It was a letter. . . .

"'Dear Becky,' it read. 'You have been on my mind and heart a lot because I know you are hurting.' The letter contained a poem, 'I Am Waiting, Lord,' about having faith through difficult times. 'Lord, help me not to simply sit among my broken things,' one line read. 'Teach me in my waiting to find the valued remnants. . . .'

"Even though I was not the person originally intended to receive this letter, I believe I was meant to see it. I do hope the other Becky got as much encouragement from it as I have. Thanks so much . . . Becky."

Slowly, I unfolded the other letter in the envelope, the one the writer had mentioned. And I did recognize the person who wrote this one. It was signed "Val Ripka." Me.

I had sent that letter to my friend Becky when she was going through a rough time in her life. It had comforted her back then, ten years earlier. She had thanked me for it when she'd received it, but later had told me that she had long since lost it, not sure where it might have gone.

Until it was found by just the right person, at just the right time.

A PLACE FOR MOM

Anna Lou McNeill

I'd tried to put the decision off as long as possible, but now my eighty-seven-year-old mom's health was failing, and she couldn't live alone anymore. She was adamant about not hiring anyone to come stay with her, and she didn't want to move out to the country to live with my husband and me. That left me with the option of finding her a nursing facility. Most of them seemed large and impersonal.

It won't be the same as home, I fretted.

My decision was all the more agonizing because Mom had worked so hard to make our two-story white house at 386 East Water Street a good home for my sister, brother and me when we were growing up. After our father, a mailman, died when I was twelve, Mom was determined to support us and hold on to the house.

"Things may be a little different without Dad," she said one night, gathering us in her downstairs bedroom with the big bay window. "But this will always be our home." Mom learned to drive and took over Dad's rural mail route. Only years later, when I'd grown up and married, did Mom sell the house.

After all she'd done for us, I couldn't imagine having Mom spend her last years in a strange new place. But she couldn't stay where she was. When my daughter offered to visit the local social services department to research nursing facilities in town, I agreed. She came back with a short list of options.

"The one that sounded best to me was a private residence that takes only three clients," my daughter said. "Do you want to go check it out?"

I knew immediately that it would be the perfect place for Mom. The staff was kind and attentive, and a first-floor bedroom with a bay window was available. We moved her in that same day, and until she passed away, Mom always referred to it as her "home sweet home." And, indeed, it was—the very same house where she had raised my sister, brother and me, 386 East Water Street.

MY OLD CEDAR CHEST

Mary Frances Williams

I sat up in bed and tried to clear my head. I dreamed I was visiting an older woman who said her name was Pearl. There in her living room was my old cedar chest. It had a sad history.

I hadn't laid eyes on that chest in more than thirty years. I would have recognized it anywhere, though. The simple lines, the delicate hinges, the clear finish that protected the beauty of the wood.

My father came from a long line of woodworkers. They had a tradition of welcoming each new baby in the family with a handmade cedar chest. Dad's uncle had hewn the cedar and crafted the chest just for me. It stood at the foot of my bed, a constant reminder to me of how much I was loved.

Then my parents had a bitter divorce, and Dad took my brothers to live with him. He threw their clothes into the chest and carried it out the door. With it, it seemed, went my best childhood memories.

Come on, Frances, I told myself. *Forget the dream. You've got to get to work.*

I was a volunteer services coordinator, and I'd booked a gospel choir from out of town to perform at our local hospital. I got there early to greet the choir. The members filed in. I could hardly believe my eyes—there was the woman from my dream!

"This is going to sound odd," I said to her. "I had a dream last night . . . and you were in it."

She smiled. "Really?"

I couldn't resist asking, "Your name wouldn't be Pearl, would it?"

Her eyes widened. "My name *is* Pearl."

"I was visiting you. You had a small chest sitting in your living room . . ."

"What did it look like?" Her expression turned serious.

"Natural cedar. Simple. Small hinges. Beautiful, clear finish. My dad took it with him when he left my mother."

She touched my arm. "Was your dad Earnest?"

"How did you know?"

"Your father was my cousin. One day he came by and gave me the chest for safekeeping. I held onto it all these years. Now I know why."

TRULY TRUDE

Kurt Weishaupt

It's been more than fifty years since my wife, Trude, and I fled to America from Europe, and to this day I'm still humbled not only that we made it out of the Holocaust, but also that we made it together.

As a German Jew, I knew I had to flee when the Nazis came to power. So in 1935, I leaped at the opportunity for a job transfer to Milan, Italy. My fiancée, Trude, followed me, and we were married there.

Soon we had to move again, this time to Nice, France. In September 1939, war exploded in Europe, and I was interned in a concentration camp. Trude was ill so she escaped internment. As I was taken away, I slipped her the name and address of a business associate in Marseilles, Mr. Biechele. "We will communicate through him," I said.

After eleven months in the camp, I was supposed to be moved to North Africa to build a railroad. On the train, however, some of the other prisoners and I were able to jump out of the car near the Spanish border. Dodging machine-gun fire, we leaped into a river and swam to safety. During the next three weeks, I made my way to Marseilles. Finally I showed up on Mr. Biechele's doorstep, desperate for some news of my wife.

"Have you heard from Trude?" I asked.

"Not once in all this time," he said.

Just as I was about to leave there was a sharp knock at the door. It was not the authorities, but the postman. He handed Mr. Biechele a postcard—from Trude! She was in Carcassonne, a town I had passed through on my way to Marseilles. I phoned her, and two days later she joined me. God was ready to take us to America on the next step of our new life together.

$\mathcal{L}$IGHT IN THE MIST

Helen Blide

$\mathcal{R}$ain pattered down on the car as my daughter, Lisa, and I crossed the border from New York into Sussex County in New Jersey. We were on our way home from visiting my mother. A cardboard box slid back and forth on the backseat. Mom had insisted we take what looked like several meals' worth of her delicious home-cooked Polish food. "Share it with your friends," Mom suggested. That was my immigrant mother. She never forgot the years our family had struggled when I was growing up and was always thinking of other families who might need help too.

"Hey," Lisa said, sitting up beside me. "Sussex County. Isn't this where Martha lives?"

"This is the place," I said sadly. My friend's warm, friendly face seemed to rise up before my eyes, as if she were right there with us. "But I don't know where exactly."

Losing Martha was one of the most painful things in my life. When she lived down the road, the two of us saw each other all the time. We worked out together to keep in shape, went antique shopping, talked about our children.

Martha had two, a boy and a girl. When her marriage broke up, she and the children moved, but I thought I wouldn't let distance come between us. I wanted to give them all the support I could. Sometimes Martha felt like more than a friend—more like the sister I had never had.

The rain stopped, replaced by a swirling mist. I'd made this trip a hundred times. I knew where I was going. *Martha's somewhere out in that mist,* I thought as I turned on my high beams. *I just don't know where.*

On an ordinary afternoon about a year before, I'd dropped by the farm where Martha lived as a caretaker to say hi. The place was empty. A sign announced the farm had been sold. Martha was gone—no forwarding address, no good-bye. Nothing. Rumor around town said she'd moved to Sussex County, but I'd never been able to track her down.

I slowed the car as I approached a fork in the road. *God,* I asked, *watch over Martha. If she needs my help, let her get in touch!*

I prepared for a right turn and stopped. *What's that?* I thought, peering through the windshield. A bright beam of light cut through the mist in the distance. I had to follow it.

I took the left fork.

"Mom, where are we going?" Lisa asked. "This isn't the way home."

"I know," I said. "But I have the strangest feeling that Martha lives right around here somewhere."

The light led us down a dead-end road. We came out of the mist. In front of us stood an old white stucco farmhouse with a red barn.

"Do you think this is it?" asked Lisa.

"Yes," I said. "I do." But how could I possibly know that? I'd never seen this farm before in my life. All those trips to visit Mom, and I'd never once wondered what was down the other fork in the road. Could it really be Martha? "You stay in the car," I told Lisa. "I'll make sure we're at the right place."

I knocked. A little girl opened the door. Blonde pigtails coming loose, a smudged face and sad blue eyes. Her brother came up behind her. "Helen!" he said. "I'm glad you're here. I think Mom could use a friend right now."

I could see dirty dishes stacked in the sink. A pile of laundry in the corner. The house was cold. It smelled musty. *This isn't like Martha.*

"Mom's in the barn."

"Stay here with the kids," I told Lisa. I hurried to the barn, my boots sinking in the mud. Faster and faster, as if I might be too late. *Too late for what?*

I pushed open the door. *Martha!* She was standing on the upper level of the barn, looking down at the piles of hay below her. Martha's back was to me. Bits of straw stuck to her green sweater and uncombed hair.

"Martha?" I said. "Is everything okay?"

She looked down at me. Martha's face was pale as a ghost, and she had dark circles under her eyes. She gave a sigh full of sadness and exhaustion but didn't seem able to speak.

I hurried up to put my arms around her. "Talk to me," I said, stroking her hair. "We've been friends a long time."

It took her a moment to get the words out. "Things got real bad, you see," she said. "I lost my job. I ran out of money. I didn't know what to do or where to turn. Then tonight..." She forced herself to get the words out. "I was going to do something drastic."

"Oh, Martha!" I said, holding her tight. "I'm so glad you didn't."

"Something stopped me," Martha said. She looked at me with her eyes full of wonder. "I asked God to send me an angel. And then an image of your face appeared in my mind."

"I'm not an angel," I said. "But it was an angel who led me to this farmhouse tonight."

I walked Martha back to the house, where Lisa and I unpacked Mom's delicious food. Martha's family would have a good dinner tonight. Then we could start work on those dishes and the laundry.

Martha's life changed for the better soon afterward. She got a new job, a new house—she even fell in love. She moved again, all the way to Florida. But this time she left me an address and phone number, and promised she would call if she ever needed anything or just wanted to talk. I was ready to listen. What's more, so was God.

$\mathcal{S}$UMMER OF '69

Judith Ann Perry

$\mathcal{W}$e had just been transferred to the naval base at Port Hueneme, California, in the fall of 1968 when my husband was deployed to Vietnam. Our son, Brad, was eight years old. He put up a brave front, but I worried how he would get along with his father so far away. We wrote letters to him every day and waited for his replies. Opening that envelope addressed to Brad and me was the highlight of our week.

Our first Christmas alone passed quietly. Almost too quietly—I noticed Brad seemed kind of subdued. Then someone from church organized a clothing and toy drive for Vietnamese war orphans. The idea really took hold of Brad and after the New Year we put his outgrown clothes, along with some toy trucks, into a box.

I was about to seal it up when Brad said, "Wait, Mom!" He rummaged through the clean laundry and took out his prized possession—the velvety blue seersucker shirt he wore everywhere. It had an ink spot on the left shoulder, but from playing to sleeping Brad practically lived in that shirt.

"You sure you want to give that away, honey?" I asked.

Brad laid the shirt on top of the pile. "I want someone in Vietnam to have it," he said, smoothing the soft blue cotton, "someone closer to Dad."

We shipped our box, and months passed. One week that summer of 1969 we received a letter addressed only to Brad. "Dear Son," Brad read aloud to me. "A few of us went to an orphanage near Quang Tri this morning. I met a little boy about your age. He wore the bluest seersucker shirt. Exactly the same as yours, except there was a stain on the left shoulder—looked like ink or grease or something. Still, when I hugged the boy good-bye, the shirt felt just as wonderfully soft as yours. Sure made me feel you were quite close today. I miss you and your mother very much."

Once Brad finished reading the letter, Vietnam didn't seem so far away anymore. And neither did his father.

"How Can I Help?"

Mary Smith

Christmas was just a few weeks away, and I strolled through the department store, picking up a few items for someone special. Every year I pick a needy child's wish list from the "Angel Tree" at my local mall, hoping to spread a little of the holiday spirit.

Wristwatch, check. A pair of athletic shoes, size six, check. Finally, I grabbed a yellow fleece jacket off the rack and brought everything to the register. It made me feel good picturing that little boy on Christmas Day, his eyes lighting up as he opened his presents. I paid the cashier and decided to take the gifts home to wrap them myself, planning on returning to the mall that night to leave them at the drop-off spot. *Just a few more errands to run first,* I thought.

The day flew by, and I arrived home much later than I expected. I felt absolutely beat. I barely touched my dinner. I went to bed early. The next morning I woke up with a fever. The flu. *Oh no. Not now…*

It was days before I could resume my Christmas preparations. The Angel Tree! I completely forgot to drop off the gifts! I hopped in the car and sped to the mall, praying that it wasn't too late. But when I got there, the tree was gone. The deadline to drop off gifts had passed. My heart sank. I turned and headed back home. *That poor child won't get anything for Christmas this year, and it's all my fault!*

That Sunday I was sitting in church listening to the prayer requests when a woman mentioned a grandmother who was raising her grandson by herself and couldn't afford any gifts for Christmas. *Could this be my chance to make up for what I did?* I thought.

I went up to the woman afterward. "How can I help?" I asked.

"She put her grandson's Christmas wish list on the Angel Tree, but they still haven't received anything," she said.

Right away I perked up. *Could it be?* "What did he ask for?"

"A wristwatch, a pair of athletic shoes, size six, and a warm jacket, in his favorite color, yellow," she said.

$\mathcal{S}$OMEONE BREEZED BY

Michael Bugeja

$\mathcal{I}$ was getting into my car near the intramural field at Oklahoma State University, where I taught journalism, when I noticed a pale band of skin on my left ring finger. My wedding ring. I'd lost it!

I had gone for one of my vigorous walks. Not strictly a field, the sprawling acreage included three miles of sloping wooded trails and even a cow pasture. The ring must have slipped off my finger while I walked.

Suddenly, finding the fourteen-karat gold band was more important than anything else on my busy schedule that afternoon. Maybe I hadn't even lost it on my walk. *I should start by checking with the campus lost and found,* I told myself. But I felt a sense of urgency that defied logic.

In easier times, my wife, Diane, and I took walks together at this field. We talked about our love and the children we desperately wanted (though could not bring into the world). More and more these days, in the spring of 1982, we took our walks separately. With my class schedule and her work as a photojournalist, our paths crossed less frequently. It felt as if we were losing sight of each other and our dreams.

It's got to be here somewhere, I thought, anxiously retracing my steps. I searched all afternoon. That evening when I told Diane, she shook her head and sighed.

"I'll find it," I promised.

Diane fell asleep early while I gazed out the bedroom window at the full moon. *Good, there will be enough light on the paths to glitter on gold.*

I parked my car at the main entrance. The air was scented with honeysuckle, and a falling mist cast mysterious hoops of moonlight. But I took little notice of the velvety beauty of the night. I was worried about my marriage. At least I was doing *something*—walking, kneeling, crawling. It was all I could do. At the time I had little faith in people to help me, and not much in God.

Toward dawn I went home to shower, empty-handed. I left a note for Diane—"No luck"—and drove back to campus to teach my classes. During breaks I checked with the lost and found. I called the local papers to see if anyone had placed an ad for a found ring. No one had.

That afternoon I returned to the intramural field, planning to search every square inch of the path on my knees if necessary. I didn't notice any cars in the sunny parking lot. Everyone was in class. I covered twenty yards or so, descending a slope between buttes. At the base of the slope was a copse of scrub oak; the path rose steeply on the other side. There was no wind or birdsong that day—just intense silence.

And then a sudden presence. Someone breezed by me. I did not see a shadow or feel footsteps on the soft earth. He wore a shiny black track suit with pink and yellow stripes. I assumed it was a man because of the tall, oblong physique, stretched thin like a reflection in a fun-house mirror. He wore a black wool cap despite the warm Okie sun. As he streaked away from me, down the slope, the sound of his words should have been faint, rippling away. But in a voice clear and distinct, I heard, "There's your ring."

A short way in front of me, in the middle of the path, on ground I had covered numerous times, gold glinted in the sun. *How could I have missed it?* Stooping, I quickly slipped my wedding band back on my finger.

I stood and waited for the man to emerge from the scrub oaks at the base of the slope and run up the opposite incline and into view. I wanted to shout a thank-you.

But he did not reappear. I ambled down to the copse. No sign of him. No tracks. No sound. I went back to the car and waited. He never returned.

Years later the memory remains, in many ways stronger now. Back then, few people spoke about angels—especially professors. I was so happy to have my ring back that I readily dismissed the odd little miracle as an earthbound coincidence, a man randomly whizzing by me as I searched the dirt path on my knees. But life has since taught me to see things differently. For starters, I'm humble enough to accept what I can't explain, and to appreciate daily blessings.

I wish I could say the mysterious jogger immediately restored my faith and rescued our marriage. In truth, all that really happened that day was that I got my wedding ring back. Yet in the years that followed, as Diane and I grew through our difficulties, my faith and our marriage would revive, and God's gifts would be countless—including a daughter and a son, whom we are now rearing in Ohio.

I had wandered those paths back in Oklahoma without a sense of purpose or direction. Today I know that the mysterious runner helped not just to retrieve something precious, but also to blaze the way to God's plan for me.

LAUNDRY DAY

Lura Cox Brand

I was desperate. My washing machine had quit right in the middle of a load of clothes I was planning to pack up and take on vacation, and I couldn't get anyone to repair it before we left.

"Come out today?" asked the sixth repairman I called. "You've got to be kidding!"

If only Dad were here now. He could fix anything. But my father had passed away recently. *Lord, help me get along without him,* I prayed. I then tried one last number.

"I'll be right over," the repairman said, once I explained to him how dire my predicament was.

True to his word, he showed up half an hour later. I couldn't thank him enough for bailing me out.

"I know what it's like," he said. "Once, I'd been laid off and we were down to our last dime, with nothing to feed the kids. All morning I drove around town looking for a job. Finally I saw a man working on a fence. He said, 'If you help me finish this, I'll give you half the pay.' Thanks to him, my kids had a good meal that night." After the repairman finished his work and the washing machine was running again, he mused, "I always wanted to be able to do something for that man, T. E. Cox."

"You just did," I said, amazed. "I'm his daughter."

"I Have No Family"

Larkin Huey

Back during the Vietnam War, when I was stationed in Thailand, I met a beautiful Thai woman named Surapun. We fell in love and got married soon after. After a doctor told my wife that she couldn't have children, we both prayed that somehow God would change things, that we would be able to have a family of our own.

My tour ended, and I went back to the United States, to my assignment in Nevada. I started the huge amount of immigration paperwork necessary for Surapun to join me back in the States.

A short time later I received a letter from Surapun. She was pregnant! The doctor had been wrong. We were ecstatic. I couldn't wait till she joined me. I rushed the paperwork to her for her signature.

A long time went by with no response. Letters I sent to her went unanswered. I was getting frantic. Then a letter came from her mother, telling me my wife had died. I was devastated. I didn't know what to do. I didn't have the money for airfare back to Thailand to pay my respects. I hadn't known my in-laws well, and soon I fell out of touch. I vowed someday I would return to Thailand. Eventually, I moved on with my life. I remarried and had two children. I earned a master's in psychology. Later I became a writer. It was nearly thirty years till I went back to Thailand.

After searching many official records, I found my wife's grave. Alone with my memories I stood beside it and prayed. Just then a young Thai woman walked up. She put her hands together in the *wye* position, a Thai gesture of respect. "Did you know her?" I asked her.

"No," she said. "But I am the reason she's dead. It weighs heavy on my mind. I have no family. They all died. And when I feel lonely I come here."

"Why here?" I asked.

"She died while giving birth to me. I have spent my life searching for my father, but he is American, and I think he doesn't want to be found."

Now, after so long, there I stood with my daughter Sirikit, an answer to a thirty-year-old prayer.

Early Morning Announcement

Loraine Stayer

This is a hard night for me, Lord. I was saying my evening prayers, looking out the window, watching a tree sway back and forth. I should've been long asleep like my husband, but how could I relax? Our daughter Miriam was at a hospital two states away, about to give birth to her first child.

Like any other grandmother-to-be, I was filled with excitement and butterflies. I wished I knew how she was doing moment by moment, but since Miriam and her husband follow a strict Jewish tradition, they don't use the phone on holy days. *Just my luck it's a holy day!* I thought. And I'd certainly pestered the nurses enough. I'd just have to wait it out and have faith that everything would work out okay.

I sat down on my bed. *God,* I whispered, *give me strength and peace of mind to fall asleep tonight.* By morning I would learn all about my beautiful new grandbaby and hear about the birth from my daughter. What would it be, a boy or a girl? Just so mother and baby were healthy, that's what mattered.

I slipped under the covers and glanced at the answering machine. *Don't even look at it,* I told myself. I closed my eyes and took a deep breath.

But what was this? I found myself sitting in my dining room. I had to be dreaming. That was it. But everything seemed so real. Suddenly an angel appeared before me. There was no question as to his nature. He had no wings but wore a yarmulke. A long, bright scroll unfurled in his hands, and he sang out, "You have a grandson."

I woke up with a start and looked around the dark bedroom. The clock radio read 5:00 AM. My husband slept soundly beside me. I pulled the covers up to my chin, thinking how tremendously beautiful that voice was.

"The voice of an angel," I murmured. Was his announcement true? Somehow I felt that mother and baby were fine. As I drifted off to sleep again, I heard the phone ring. The answering machine picked up. The same wonderful voice again sang, "You have a grandson."

How nice of the hospital to call, I thought. I was elated. In my sleepy state, I supposed all good news sounded as if it came from an angel!

When I woke up later that morning, I checked the message. There was no message at all. I looked down at the red, flashing zero. *Of course there's no message,* I realized. *You were dreaming. Since when do hospitals leave singing messages on people's machines?*

Soon we learned my healthy grandson had been born at exactly five o'clock in the morning. My daughter was doing just fine. Grandmother, never better! Surely this had been a holy day.

Steinway in New York

A. Samuel Mattson

Jobs were hard to find in New York City in 1930. Just nineteen, I was fresh off the boat from Sweden and didn't speak any English.

When I'd boarded the train in my hometown of Karlskrona, Sweden, a woman next to me had asked, "Where are you going?"

"America," I said. "To make a new start."

"My cousin Lars works in New York City," she informed me. "At the Steinway piano factory. Look him up when you get there." She wrote on a piece of paper, handed it to me and said, "God be with you."

It was a sweltering New York day when I set out in search of the factory. I had no idea where it was. I wandered the city for hours, showing people that scrap of paper, which bore four words: "Lars Olsen—Steinway Piano." Nobody was able to help me.

I was disappointed, and so tired. When I saw a parked car I opened the door and slid into the front seat. Where I was from anyone could rest in someone else's wagon or cart. I hoped the same was true here.

I soon fell asleep but was jolted awake by the blast of a whistle. Workmen streamed out of a nearby building. One of them yelled at me, in English. *What is he so upset about?* I answered instinctively in Swedish that I was sorry. Amazingly, he responded in Swedish, "What are you doing in my car?" I explained, and then showed him that piece of paper. The man smiled. He said the whistle I had heard announced the end of the workday at Steinway & Sons. Then he walked me around the corner and introduced me to someone who got me a job as a painter.

By now you've probably guessed. The man who owned the car was Lars Olsen.

For You?

Robert McCormick

Sweaty palms, dry mouth, a voice sure to crack. In my first year of training to become a deacon, I dreaded reading from Scripture. Unfamiliar biblical names and places could be impossible to pronounce at first glance, but I was at a loss for what to do. I was a college teacher with three young children, so I rarely had time to practice the daily readings in the book kept at the parish house.

One day I was walking with Father Elmer, our parish priest. "I wish I had my own copy of the daily readings so I could study in my spare time," I confessed.

"That would help," he replied, "but copies are hard to come by."

Up ahead a man waited. "You probably don't remember me, Father Elmer," he said, "but I used to be in your congregation." He'd moved away, he explained, and was only visiting. "I wonder if you know someone who could use this." The man handed Father Elmer a book and we continued on our way. As he sat down at his desk in the parish house, Father Elmer took a closer look at the book. "Here," he said, "I think this is for you."

I leafed through it. January 27, March 22, July 17 …the readings for every day of the year! I'd found the very thing I'd been looking for—or, should I say, the very thing found me.

· 3 ·

GIVING AID

HAVE MERCY ON ME, O LORD,
FOR I AM IN TROUBLE. . . .
—*Psalm 31:9*

Lord, increase my faith through the witness of these stories—people you have rescued in the face of distress or danger.

BALED OUT

Joan Engelhardt Nielsen

In the summer of 1993, rain deluged the Midwest. Here in Jackson County, Iowa, farms were flooded, the hay crop ruined. There was enough feed to last through autumn, but how would we provide for our livestock come winter?

Cold weather set in, and the hay mangers remained bare. Cattle died. Our neighbors went bankrupt. Families suffered.

Then farmers in Pennsylvania heard about our plight and donated hay. One thousand four hundred forty bales were on the way by rail, each one an answer to prayer. I joined the committee that handled people's applications for free hay. I knew every one of the eighteen farmers who signed up.

The day the bales came, everyone pulled up their hay wagons to the rail yard. Men climbed into the box-cars and tossed fresh hay down to their neighbors. I carefully counted bales—1,440 bales, eighteen farmers, eighty bales each.

A little old pickup drove up. An elderly man I didn't recognize got out. "This where we get the free hay?" he asked. "I'm going to have to sell my horses if I don't find some."

I can't ask the others to give up some of their hay. Eighty bales will barely get them through the week.

It nearly broke my heart to tell the elderly farmer all the hay was spoken for.

"I might as well stick around and lend a hand," he said, and jumped into a boxcar.

Lord, can't you do something for this man? I asked.

Finally all the wagons were filled. "There's some hay left!" someone yelled from one of the boxcars.

The old farmer's eyes lit up. We piled the extra hay into the bed of his pickup. There was room for fourteen bales—the exact amount that was left over.

Just goes to show that no matter how great the number, no matter how great the need, the Lord always provides.

We're Not Going to Make It

Wilda Lahmann

My husband, Randy, shook me awake. It must have been 2:00 AM. He was hunched over, holding a hand to his chest. "Wilda, I need to get to the hospital," he said, gasping. "Can't breathe."

"I'll call 911," I said, jumping out of bed.

"No time," he gasped again. "Drive me. Now."

I helped him up and got him out to our van. Randy slumped against the passenger-side door. Fifteen miles to the hospital. *Too far,* I thought. *We're not going to make it. Send help, Lord.*

We tore out of the driveway, engine roaring in the still night air. Could Randy hold on? About a mile down the road, at the bottom of a hill, I saw something in the street. Were my eyes playing tricks on me? No, it was real. An ambulance!

"Look, Randy!" I shouted. A paramedic stood outside the vehicle. Was he waiting for us? Who could have known to call?

I slammed on the brakes, leaped out of the van and ran over to the ambulance, screaming for help. The paramedic and his partner went right to work. "Possible cardiac," one said. They strapped an oxygen mask onto Randy and started treatment. Then they loaded him onto a stretcher and into the ambulance, unconscious. "Follow us," one of them instructed.

The next three days were touch-and-go. I never left Randy's bedside, praying he'd wake up. Finally, he did. "What happened?" he asked.

"You mean you don't remember?"

"Nothing after the ambulance," he said.

"You had a massive heart attack. The EMTs said another minute or two and . . ." I squeezed his hand tight.

"You called them?" Randy asked.

"No," I told him. "They received a report of a car crash at that intersection. They even called in to make sure that they were at the right location. They were. And then we came along seconds later."

Fifteen miles on empty roads in the middle of the night. Randy's heart attack *would* have been fatal if those paramedics hadn't been there. I'd say they were in the perfect location.

LATE ONE RAINY NIGHT

Marcus M. Silverman

Not a good night to be out," I muttered to myself, watching the rain roll off the awning in front of me. It never failed. The second I got far away from my apartment, it started pouring. Normally I'd just wait it out under one of those dripping awnings, but it was one o'clock in the morning and I had work the next day. The walk was supposed to clear my head, but the humid spring night had made me sticky, wet and tired. I wasn't in a terrible mood, but I'd been blue recently, that's for sure. My father had been diagnosed with one of the more dangerous strains of skin cancer. It was the first time in my life that my father's mortality had really struck me and I was scared. My apartment in Brooklyn, New York, was small and crowded, and I'd developed cabin fever at night. Long, reflective walks usually helped.

Too bad this wasn't a night to be out walking. I saw a subway station across the street and splashed over to escape the rain. Much better to ride the train three stops back to my neighborhood. I descended the steps and took out my fare card as I shook the water out of my hair and swiped through the turnstile.

There was only one other person on the platform with me—a man in his early thirties with a blue baseball cap. Since it was only me and him on the platform, I assumed that we'd just missed a train and I slunk down to the far end of the platform and sat on the wooden bench, staring off into space. *Boy,* I thought to myself, *I'm in a blue, blue mood: soaking wet, sitting on an uncomfortable bench, underground.* I scuffed my shoes against the dirty concrete. *Why my dad?*

A low moaning, almost a wailing, came from the man with the cap. *Great. Just what I need.* The man stumbled toward me. My antipathy turned quickly into concern.

"Hey, buddy," I asked, getting up from the bench, "are you okay?" The man let out another loud, pained moan and collapsed onto the ground. I ran and knelt next to him. He appeared to be unconscious, but his eyes were open. Blood trailed from his mouth and his arm was bent in a strange position. I ran for the station attendant on the other side of the turnstile—no cell-phone reception underground.

"Police or ambulance?" The station agent asked before I'd said a word.

"A man has passed out," I said. "He needs an ambulance." The attendant unclipped her radio from her shirt and spoke with her dispatch.

I heard the telltale beep of a fare card being swiped. A man in a white doctor's coat came through the turnstile. "Excuse me," I sputtered, "are you a doctor?"

"Yes," he said, "a surgeon."

I explained what happened as we jogged toward the felled man on the platform. The surgeon leaned over him and felt his pulse. "It appears to be an epileptic seizure," he said, unbuttoning the man's shirt around his collar. "The fall is probably what injured his arm. He should be fine though."

The doctor used his handkerchief to make a sling for the unconscious man. I breathed a sigh of relief and leaned against the brick wall. "He's sure lucky you showed up," I said as the doctor sat the man up against the wall. *More than lucky,* I thought. In fact, I'd never seen such perfect timing. I took a good look at this in-the-right-place, at-the-right-time doctor. He *did* have an odd look about him—that pristine white coat in this filthy subway station. He smiled at me as he held the man's head up slightly. "I'm Gregory, from Metro Hospital up the street."

I asked him what kind of medicine he practiced and he said, "Dermatological surgery, mainly." I shook my head. *Just the kind of surgeon Dad needs.* "Do you do melanoma surgeries?" I blurted out, half-embarrassed. He nodded and gave me a sympathetic glance as if he knew everything I was worried about. I was eager to ask him a bunch of questions, but I heard the wheels of a stretcher rolling toward us. The paramedics had arrived. Gregory and I watched in silence as they lifted the injured man onto the stretcher. He moved his head and his eyes fluttered. He was regaining consciousness now. I felt a comforting touch.

"Well, Marcus," Gregory smiled, "I guess I'm not done for the night after all. I should go over to the hospital with these guys." We shook hands, and I thanked him for being such a Good Samaritan. An angel even. He looked at me warmly. "Something tells me your father is going to be all right," he said, and with that he turned on his heel and followed the paramedics up the stairs to the street.

I looked down the empty tunnel. Still no train. My heart had finally stopped thumping. *Too much excitement for tonight*, I thought. Suddenly I sucked in my breath and my heart started pounding again, even louder than before: *"Well, Marcus,"* the surgeon had said. My mind was going a mile a minute. *I had never told him my name or mentioned that it was my father I was worried about.* I tore off running toward the exit after the paramedics and Gregory, almost tripping over myself in the process.

Aboveground I saw the paramedics about to take off. "Where'd that doctor go?" I practically screamed. The EMTs looked at one another and then back at me, confused. "The doctor. The surgeon," I repeated. "In the white coat. He works at Metro Hospital up the street."

The paramedics just stared at me blankly. "Kid," one of them said, "I've been an EMT for nine years. There's no Metro Hospital in Brooklyn." He turned to slam the door to the ambulance and it sped off.

The rain had stopped. *Your father is going to be all right,* the mysterious surgeon had said. And he was right. A year later my father is cancer free. But I'll never forget that late-night encounter with a surgeon in a white coat. I'd left my apartment on a humid spring night to find my peace of mind. I got it. And a whole lot more.

MAYDAY

Hilary Hemingway

My father was a commercial fisherman when I was young and he had to spend long weeks at sea. One day shortly after I'd turned ten, he was scheduled to be off the coast of Jamaica. We were at our home in Miami. Mom was washing the dinner dishes when her face drained of color. "Mayday," she whispered.

Without even wiping her hands, Mom grabbed the phone. She called the Coast Guard and told the man on duty that she was concerned about her husband.

"Yes, ma'am, we know your husband sure did run into some trouble," he replied. "They're having a heavy storm and he radioed in for help when his boat started taking in water. We flew out there about an hour ago and dropped him a heavy-duty bilge pump."

"I don't believe that the pump is working," Mom insisted. "You need to do another fly-over."

The man tried to placate Mom. "He must be all right, Mrs. Hemingway, or we would've heard from him."

"You haven't gotten a Mayday?"

"No, but we'll let you know if we hear anything." Mom hung up. Without saying a word, she went into her bedroom and knelt by her bed. An hour passed. Mom came out, looking even more anxious. She called the Coast Guard again. This time she had steel in her voice. "You had better send a plane out right now or you'll be retrieving the bodies of Leicester Hemingway and his crew."

They said they would send out a rescue plane as soon as possible.

Mom was awake that whole night praying. Early in the morning the phone rang. It was the Coast Guard. They had found my father and his crew floating in debris fifteen miles off Jamaica. Dad's boat had sunk, but all were safe.

Dad arrived home that same afternoon, weary and sunburnt. "The bilge pump they dropped didn't work fast enough," he said. "Too much water was coming in. It started pouring over our transom. I radioed in a Mayday, but my call never got through."

But it had—to Mom.

Saved by the Bell

Pearl Maurer

I was gardening one afternoon at our summer cottage on Lake Ontario. I'd grabbed a clump of weeds near an old tree trunk when I suddenly recoiled. Too late. Out swarmed a squad of angry bees. I got a nasty sting on my hand—I had forgotten my gloves.

I yanked out the stinger and rushed toward the cottage for ice, but I didn't get far. Nausea and dizziness swept over me, and then I had trouble breathing. *I'm having a reaction. I've got to get help.* My husband was working and the kids were in town with their friends. I glanced across the yard to see if my neighbor Donna was around. No car in the driveway, no sign of anyone home.

My whole arm was swelling now and my joints ached. Only a rising sense of panic kept me moving. *Maybe Donna's parents are home.* Their cottage was right behind Donna's. I staggered out of the yard, past two driveways. *I'm not going to make it.* I tried to shout. No words came out. I made it to the porch steps, praying, *Somebody be home. Please hear me!*

The last thing I remember was reaching for the doorbell. When I came to, people were hovering around me. "She's DOA," one said. *No, I'm not!* I thought before slipping back into unconsciousness.

I awoke in a hospital bed with a doctor standing over me. He looked relieved. I glanced around the room. There were Donna, my husband and the kids. "Good thing you got here when you did, Mrs. Maurer," the doctor said. "Another few minutes and you wouldn't have survived that allergic reaction to the bee sting. You went into anaphylactic shock."

The doctors kept me overnight for observation. In the morning, Donna came by to fill in the gaps in my memory. "You rang my parents' bell and then collapsed. They told me they heard the bell and came running."

"Thank God they did!"

"That's the odd part. They're both almost completely deaf. They haven't been able to hear that doorbell in years."

SNOW ANGELS

Myra McNair

The impending snowstorm was all over the news that week. By Friday there was a warning in effect and people were stocking up on milk, bread, toilet paper, as though they'd never get to the store again. I was actually looking forward to a quiet snowbound weekend with my fourteen-year-old daughter, Tia. Then I heard the latest forecast: up to forty-eight inches of snow in less than twenty-four hours. Four feet was way more than Tia and I could shovel!

Friday night the snow began to fall, covering the lawn. Then the street. Soon, a blanket of white covered everything. Our pastor had talked about how God cares about our smallest needs. Well, I had some needs now and they didn't seem so small. I stood at the storm door. "Dear Father," I prayed out loud, "you said that you put your angels in charge over us. Please send some angels to help us with all this snow!"

"What are you doing?" Tia asked.

"You'll see," I said. "God is going to send someone to shovel our walk."

Tia laughed. "If it's the two boys next door, it really will be a miracle!" They never even helped shovel their *own* walk. And it wouldn't be our neighbor on the other side. He'd thrown his back out. Maybe some enterprising teens would show up in the morning.

Tia and I settled in for the night. Just before I fell asleep, I peeked out the bedroom window. Snow was piling up. There had to be two feet already because I couldn't even see my car's tires anymore. Whomever God sent would need a snow blower.

First thing in the morning I looked out the window again. The drifts were five feet high in places. Cars were almost completely covered. Snow was everywhere. Everywhere except on our walk and driveway. Our car was completely clear, as if someone had brushed every flake away.

"Tia, you've got to see this!" I called, and then dashed down the stairs and threw open the front door. Even the welcome mat was free of snow. "I don't believe it!" I couldn't even see a single footprint.

"You said that angels would clear our path," Tia reminded me.

Tia was right: snow angels! Who else could have done all this work?

$\mathscr{A}$ FLASH OF WHITE

Dana Christmas

$\mathcal{W}$ay to go! I called to a friend down the hall. "Happy New Year!" Closing the door to my dorm room I smiled, glad to be back at Seton Hall University. That January night two years ago, we'd been celebrating a great beginning to the semester: Our basketball team had just beaten our No. 1 rival, St. John's University. They'd always slammed us before, but that night we'd kicked their butts. "Yes!" I said, spinning around in my room, feeling triumphant.

I'd come back to campus after Christmas break at home with my family in Paterson, about forty-five minutes away. Mom had wanted me to stay longer, as always, but I was excited to start the new semester. I was proud to be continuing a tradition at Seton Hall. My mom had gone there, as well as my godmother and my high school mentor. In a few months I'd graduate with a degree in criminal justice. College had gone by so fast, and being a senior seemed like a dream, especially since I was in Boland Hall, where I'd lived as a freshman. Now I was a resident manager, in charge of a hundred students in two wings of the dorm's third floor. I wasn't that much older, but I was like a den mother to these freshmen. Sometimes we'd talk in the lounge. They came to me for advice about school or dating, or just because they were lonely. Some of them helped me too, setting an example with their strong faith. I'd always gone to church, but I didn't know God like some of those kids. "He's with us," Mom would say. "You can feel his spirit." I wished I could.

Still, I said my prayers. *Where are you in my life, God?* I wondered, all cozy in bed that night. It was quiet in the dorm. I knew my friends along the third floor were also settling in before classes the next day. And we even beat St. John's. "Yes!" I switched off the light. This was going to be a great new year.

The piercing whine of the fire alarm woke me. *Oh no,* I thought, *not again.* We'd had so many false alarms that year I'd lost count. I couldn't let that stop me. It was still pitch-dark outside as I struggled out of bed. I knew most of the freshmen would turn over and go back to sleep, but it was my job to check if everything was all right. I stepped into the hall, and looked left, down the hall to our lounge. Flames blazed inside the lounge, and thick black smoke rolled through the doorway. I stood for a second in shock. *This is a fire! This is real!* Panicked, I leaped back into my room. *What do I do?* I could open the window and jump. I could race down the stairs—one of the four exit doors on the floor was next to my room. *No! I have to help my friends.* I ran into the smoky hall, screaming: "Fire!" My eyes stung with the smoke. "Fire!" I screamed again, hurrying past the lounge to the rooms beyond.

I pounded on doors along the hall. "Wake up! Get out! Fire!" Didn't anybody hear me? The smoke was choking me, and I stumbled back to my room, slamming the door. I gasped the clean air inside. My head hurt so much! My hair was sizzling. I rubbed at my scalp, trying to stop the burning. I pushed the window open. "Fire!" I screamed. "Please! Wake up!" Lights came on in windows around mine. Some kids were getting up! *Thank God!*

I had to go back to warn the others. A wall of smoke hit me in the face as I opened the door, but I ran past the lounge again. "Wake up!" I yelled, pounding like crazy on every room. Finally, doors began to open, and the kids ran toward the exits. The air was thick with smoke and screams. "Dana! You're on fire!" someone cried out.

I smacked wildly at the flames in my clothes and struggled once more to my room. A few gasps of air and I was back out in the hall. This time I turned right, pounding on doors in the other wing. "Fire!" I heard kids getting up. The smoke now covered everything like a stinking blanket. I couldn't see, but I heard kids stumbling toward the exits. My lungs burned. I couldn't stop crying. *Oh, God, help me. I'm so afraid.*

I made my way back to my room. There's clean air in there, I told myself. My hands hurt so much I couldn't feel the walls. My head throbbed. I reached the door, but my knees buckled. I had no strength left. I collapsed on the floor.

"Hold on." A man was calling to me, his words drifting through the smoke like a fresh breeze. "I'm coming for you." I glimpsed a flash of white. Then strong arms embraced me, lifting me, raising me up. As we moved slowly through the blackness I no longer felt pain. I couldn't see him, but the man held me tight. I heard a door slam, and I felt us descending a stairway, escaping into the night. The cool air swept over me.

I don't remember when I woke up, but my first thought was, *I have to get to class.* Pushing back the sheets on my bed, I groped for my sneakers.

"Dana!" my mother cried. "What are you doing?" She gently laid me down again, and I saw fear in her eyes. "Don't you know what you've been through?" I realized I was in a hospital bed. Mom told me I'd been in critical condition for several weeks—and in an induced coma to help me heal. Worst of all, I learned many freshmen had been injured in the fire, and three of my friends on the third floor hadn't made it. "Everyone else got out, Dana," Mom said. "You did everything you could." Slowly I put the pieces back together again in my mind, all except one.

My best friend told me later that the other kids thought I'd died in the fire. She saw me come down the steps to the first floor and walk out of the building alone.

"Walk?" I asked. Impossible. My doctor agreed. With the severity of my burns, I couldn't have taken another step, he said. Certainly not three flights of stairs! When I told my mother how I'd escaped, she understood immediately. "You felt his spirit," she said, and at last I knew where God was in my life. He was carrying me through it.

"CAN'T IMAGINE"

Michelle Harper

Keeping track of seven children is hard under any circumstances, so my sister, Angie, and I were on triple alert when we took all the kids to the Martin Luther King Jr. Day parade. "It's a long way back to our car," Angie said when the celebration was over. "I don't know if the little ones will make it."

"I'll wait here," I said. "Pick us up with the car."

Angie went off with my oldest son. "They'll be back soon," I assured the others, all tired, hungry and thirsty. A half hour passed and Angie was nowhere in sight. *She must have gotten lost,* I thought. *Now what?*

As if in answer, it started to rain. I herded the kids into a stucco building that housed a little cantina. "I don't have any money," I said to the man behind the counter, "but could I trouble you for some water?"

"No problem!" The man passed out paper cups of water, and then reappeared with barbecue sandwiches, pickles and chips. "It's on the house." When Angie pulled up in the car, the kids were full and checking out the jukebox.

At home I called the newspaper, hoping our story would make the parade coverage. A reporter returned my call. "Can't imagine what you're talking about, Miss. Nothing there. Nothing."

What? I drove right back. The stucco building was exactly where we'd left it. Only problem was, I couldn't get in. It was completely boarded up, abandoned for years, it looked like.

ℐNCIDENT IN IRAQ

Steven Manchester

Khaki camouflage uniform, combat boots, scarf to keep the blowing sand out of my face. I stood at my checkpoint post in the Iraqi desert, overdressed for the killer spring heat. I twirled the wedding ring on my finger. Just about the only thing I had to remind me that normal life awaited back home. You could forget that out here in the desert.

I was an Army MP, manning an outpost on Main Supply Route Blue, forty miles north of the Saudi border. This had been my assignment for a solid month in 1991, ever since the main fighting in Operation Desert Storm had ended. Troops and supply convoys still passed through, but not often. Most of the action was far to the north. I was just punching the clock, waiting for my twelve-hour shift to end so I could return to base camp to chow down and sleep.

A jeep approached from the north, the only vehicle in sight. Well, more or less in sight. A ferocious sandstorm had kicked up, obscuring the jeep from clear view. When it got close enough for me to see that it was one of ours, I waved the driver on through.

Unexpectedly, he stopped.

"Man, am I glad to see you!" he said. "I lost my convoy in the storm. Not a good thing. I'm supposed to be on Main Supply Route Green."

From the stripes on his uniform, I knew he was a sergeant like me.

"Well, you've come to the right guy," I said. "Go south for about four miles. At the fork in the road, you've met up with Green. Good luck."

The sergeant's face relaxed. "One day I hope to return the favor, buddy." With a wave, he was on his way. And I was alone again, a speck in the sand, counting the minutes till I could resume normal life back home.

Three tedious months passed. And time passed slowly in the desert. One afternoon in base camp, my platoon sergeant, Tony Rosini, drove up in a Humvee. "Got any big plans for yourself today?" he asked.

"Yeah, I'm thinking of heading out to the mall."

Tony laughed. "How about you drive me across the Saudi border instead? I want to see an army doctor about my bum knee. Besides, I could use a diversion, and from the looks of it, Manchester, so could you."

I didn't hesitate. I motioned him into the passenger seat and off we went.

Humvees can *boogie.* The wind was calm, the weather clear for a change. We had the highway to ourselves, doing sixty mph. I scanned the road for snipers. There were still Republican Guard commandos on the loose. But I wasn't worried. Not really. The bad guys seldom came out before nightfall.

Out of nowhere, a sandstorm whipped up with hurricane intensity. The blue sky turned a malevolent orange. Winds rearranged the desert landscape. Our two-lane highway disappeared. Swirling sand enveloped us completely. I imagined we were hidden from God himself.

Suddenly I heard a loud bang. *Sniper fire?* The Humvee pitched left on two wheels and spun like a hockey puck. The windshield cracked, fissures spreading like a spiderweb across the glass. My helmet flew off, and something blunt and heavy smashed into the back of my skull.

Next thing I knew, I was on my belly, forty feet from the vehicle. It had flipped upside down. The storm had died down some, and I could see. How long had I been unconscious?

Tony was hanging limp in the wreckage, tethered by his seat belt. Gas and oil leaked from the vehicle. The engine roared. *The thing could go up in flames any minute!* I had to get Tony out.

I tried to move, but my left arm and neck felt like they'd been stomped. Somehow I got up and stumbled over to the vehicle. I struggled with the seat belt and dragged Tony to safety. He was unconscious, but he had a pulse. I loosened his clothing and moistened his lips with water from my canteen. He was pretty banged up, but his life did not seem to be in danger. Not from the accident, anyway.

Through the sandstorm I made out a boulder by the apron of the highway, where the road curved. *So that's what happened.* We'd hit the boulder and careened off. The door on the driver's side had torn off and the frame was caved in, completely crushed.

Now what? Tony was too hurt to move, and I was too hurt to carry him very far. We couldn't call for help. The radio-phone antenna was buried under the Humvee. In a few hours it would be dark. Desert dark. *Great.*

"I'm freezing," Tony mumbled, finally coming around.

I rummaged through the wreckage for a blanket. I grabbed what ammo I could find—not enough to protect us for long. I put the blanket over Tony and pulled it up under his chin. That's when I noticed my wedding band was missing. It must have fallen into the sand.

That ring hadn't been off my finger since my wedding day.

I dropped to my knees and scoured the area, digging, sifting, digging, sifting, praying to find my ring, praying for someone to find us, until I sank back on my haunches in despair.

"Help's coming, isn't it?" Tony asked me. I could barely hear the question.

I gave up my search and crawled over to him. He was slipping in and out of consciousness. I cradled Tony's head in my arms. "Sure. Help's on the way," I said. *God, please don't let that be a lie.*

Drifts formed around us. The sun started to sink into the sand. I must have passed out for a moment. Because when I opened my eyes a soldier—an American soldier—was standing over me, his hand on my shoulder. He was silhouetted by the still-setting sun. "Lie down, Sarge. I'm gonna take care of you now. We're gonna get you out of here. Okay?"

I put my hand to my forehead to shield my eyes. I stared at the soldier in wonder. "It's you. . . ." The guy I'd given directions to a few months before.

"How do you like that?" he said. "I drive a scout vehicle for a medical unit. I've radioed our convoy. They'll be along in a few. Found you just in time, buddy. It's no fun out here after dark."

The medics arrived and examined Tony and me. We were going to be fine. My buddy helped strap us onto litters and lifted us aboard a medevac helicopter. "Here's something to remember me by," he said. He grabbed my hand and slapped something in it.

I looked down. In my palm was my gold wedding band, battered and speckled with sand. I slid it back onto my finger. *Normal life.* It was within my reach.

Meantime, it looked like nothing was hidden from God. Not life's smallest detail. The chopper was in the air by then. I scanned the ground looking for the sergeant, but he was gone, the favor repaid in full.

TROUBLE IN THE GULF

Roy Pitre

The life of a shrimp fisherman was hard, and lonely for a young guy like me with a new wife at home. I worked on my cousin Ulysse's boat in the Gulf of Mexico off the coast of Louisiana. One trip we'd caught lots of shrimp, but we'd been gone nine days and had another seven to go. I missed Christine. I could feel her prayers every day, joining in with my own. "Don't forget," she always said, "the angels are out there with you."

One morning that trip, after an all-nighter dragging our nets, we loaded the shrimp on board. The nets were hoisted on a nylon rope looped through steel shackles. I heard a snap. That's all I remember. I woke up lying on deck, covered in blood. Ulysse knelt beside me. "It's bad, Roy," he said. "A shackle knocked you in the head. We've got to get you stitched up."

We were thirty miles out. "We'll head to Port Fourchon," Ulysse said, "and get you to a hospital." Ulysse handed me a towel. "Hold this hard to your head." I did as he said. He steered toward land. The towel soaked with blood. I was groggy and weak. *What if I don't make it?*

"Look. A boat," Ulysse said. First one we'd seen all morning. It was a sport-fishing vessel dead in the water. A man waved a white distress flag.

We pulled up behind the boat. Six men stood on the deck. "Sorry, we can't stop," Ulysse shouted. "My cousin needs surgery." One man ran into the cabin and came out with a black bag. "I'm a surgeon," he said. "We all are! Let me aboard."

The doctor shaved my head and deadened the area around the wound. Stitched me right up. I couldn't wait to tell Christine. What were the chances that a couple of shrimpers would happen upon a boatload of surgeons in our time of need? Christine would probably say one hundred percent—if the angels are out there shrimping with you.

· 4 ·
Giving Direction

In all your ways acknowledge Him,
And He shall direct your paths.

—*Proverbs 3:6*

*Lord, lead us as we depend on you
for guidance and direction.*

MESSENGER FROM THE SKY

Rose T. Zeilman

One August evening in 1980 I stood in my front yard, silent with wonder as streaks of silvery light shot across the sky. It was the time of the annual Perseid meteor showers, and the heavens were putting on a spectacular show. "It's great being here to see this, Mom," George said, putting his arm around my waist. My son and his family had been living with me since spring. After eight years with a security job in the Air Force, he'd decided not to reenlist. He had packed everything in his Chevy truck and come home to Florida to start over as a civilian. "It'll be easier on my family," he said, and I agreed. George's father had been a career Navy man, and I worked at the Naval Air Station Jacksonville. I understood how difficult the military could be.

At first it was fun, all of us being together. The children were both only preschool age then, and always wide-eyed with discovery. We took trips to St. Augustine and other Florida sights. We shared the chores and the babysitting, and my daughter-in-law, Penney, and I kept a jigsaw puzzle going on a table in the living room. We had cookouts in the backyard—hot dogs, sweet corn, watermelon and all the trimmings. But my house was small, and I'd been used to living alone. Spring had turned into summer, and the strain was beginning to show. George's job search had taken much longer than he'd expected, and he was beginning to become filled with self-doubt. Money was tight, and getting a job, any job, became critical.

That hot August night, as the celestial rockets plunged through the sky, I said a prayer for my son, asking God for some of that heavenly power to be directed to him and his need for work.

George slipped away at one point, and I noticed him down the street talking to someone. Their conversation seemed animated, and after a few minutes they shook hands. George started back home and then turned to wave. "Thanks, Jim!"

George hurried to me. "I have a job lead!" he said. He told me the man had recently moved from Merritt Island, home of the Kennedy Space Center. "Jim said they hire civilians for security jobs, and I'm qualified." There was a look of hope on my son's face I hadn't seen for months. "I'm going to drive down there," he said, "first thing in the morning."

"But you have no appointment," I said, "and no clearance. You just can't walk into a place like the Space Center." I was afraid my son was grasping at straws.

"I've a good feeling about this, Mom," George said. "I believe Jim knew what he was talking about. Wait and see."

By six thirty the next morning George was in his Chevy truck, headed for Merritt Island. He came home that evening, triumphant. "I did it!" he said. "I'm hired!" It seemed like no less than a miracle. "I talked like I've never talked before," George explained. "I mentioned Jim, even though I didn't know his full name. I told them about the Air Force and my family and how ready I was to go to work." He stopped to catch his breath. "I guess I just talked my way inside. They gave me a guest badge, and I was directed to personnel."

In ten days George found a place for his family to live on Merritt Island, and he started his job at the Space Center. The heavens had truly been filled with power that August night. An angel named Jim arrived on a meteor.

First Things First

Sheila Revels

I had a lot on my mind that Wednesday afternoon as I rushed home from the school where I teach. I made a quick stop at the grocery store to pick up dinner, wondering all the while how I would juggle cooking, laundry and the paperwork I had that night. Just then I thought of my friend Toni. "Honey," she was fond of saying in her Southern drawl, "slow down and take one thing at a time."

That was Toni, always getting me to calm down and focus. *You're right, Toni,* I thought. I parked the van and walked into the market to buy dinner. Picking up hot dogs and buns, I hustled through the express lane and back to my van.

I put the sack of groceries and my purse on the front seat and reached out to close the van door. I was startled to see a man dressed in black with a towel over his hand blocking the door. "Excuse me," I began. To my horror, I noticed the barrel of a gun sticking out of the towel. "Let me in," he growled. Without even thinking, I pushed him hard. The gun flew to the pavement and the man scrambled after it. "Help! Help!" I screamed. My assailant raced to a nearby car and climbed in beside the waiting driver.

"Help!" I screamed again. Everything was happening too fast. *What should I do?* A few others from the parking lot rushed to me. What a surprise it was to see Toni there too! "Honey, one thing at a time," she said. "First, get that license plate number." *Of course,* I thought. I committed it to memory just as the car sped out of sight.

The store manager got the plate number from me and called the police. I looked for Toni but she'd already left. The police arrived soon after and told us the suspects had been caught based on the number I provided. At the station I identified my assailant.

When I finally got home I called Toni. "The men were caught," I said, "all because you were there to help me think straight."

"Slow down, honey," she said. "I don't know what you're talking about. I haven't left the house all day."

$\mathcal{B}$ETTER THAN EVER

Donna Ziegler

$\mathcal{O}$ur daughter, Kendra, dreamed of having a perfect wedding. When she got engaged to her college sweetheart, I was thrilled.

From a trip to India, my husband and I brought home twenty-five yards of delicate hand-spun silk for her gown. "Oh, Mom, it's beautiful!" Kendra said, gasping. "The color looks like candlelight." She had been sketching wedding-dress designs for years, and I knew how much fun we would have making sure hers was just right.

Then Kendra told me she had found a seamstress in the town where the wedding was scheduled—clear across the state. It made sense; my daughter was finishing her senior year there. Still, I felt left out.

As we planned the wedding, I questioned Kendra over every detail, right down to the color of her shoes. (She wanted orange—her fiancé's favorite hue.) "Lord, I don't want this to come between us," I prayed. "Please bring us together."

Three months before the wedding the seamstress called. "There was a fire," she said. "Kendra's dress was ruined." The silk was scorched from neckline to hem, and the gown reeked of smoke.

I had Kendra bring the dress home to our trusted dry cleaner, who soaked it for a month in a special solution. That only made the imitation pearls on the bodice melt, leaving stringy dark rings.

"I'm going to wear it anyway," Kendra insisted when I called her at school. She didn't know I had exiled the gown to our porch because of the stench.

One evening our son, Keith, stopped by. He couldn't help wrinkling his nose as he strode up the porch steps. "You know, Mom," he said. "Let's pray for Kendra's dress." And that's exactly what we did.

The next morning I woke up with a persistent thought: *Wash it by hand.* It couldn't hurt. I washed and I prayed, gently rubbing laundry detergent into each smudge with my fingertips. Then I hung the gown on our clothesline.

When it dried I couldn't believe my eyes: The scorch marks had faded! After two more hand-washings and countless prayers, every black spot vanished! The dress smelled like fresh air.

At the end of May, Kendra graduated and came home. Together we replaced the melted pearls and added five thousand more, talking quietly for the first time in months and feeling closer than we ever had. When my daughter walked down the aisle, I smiled at the orange pumps peeking from beneath her hem. Her candlelight gown wasn't the only thing that had been washed with prayer. So had our relationship.

LOST LADY ON RED MOUNTAIN

Randy Spears

I'm not the kind of guy who "sees things." I'm just a hardworking cowboy trying to get by. But late one afternoon in the High Sierras I was drawn into an adventure that still has me shaking my head.

It was a few days after Labor Day last year and I was driving my 1967 Chevy pickup home after a hard day of horseshoeing. I was feeling kind of blue because I had been struggling for so long to keep my head above water. Forty years old, with a wife and four youngsters to support (not to mention a dozen or so horses and mules), I was doing just about anything to make a nickel—trail guiding, leading pack trips, mending fences, cowboy stuff like that.

When you get out in pine-scented high country, though, and see the grandeur of our Creator, you can't feel too bad. I brightened up, and that's when it happened. I was crossing the South Fork River on a twisty little road, glancing up at a mountain towering over me, when out of nowhere the words *search and rescue* flashed hard across my mind—followed by the thought, *Maybe you can help.*

What's going on? I wondered. Was somebody in trouble? Figuring it was just my imagination, I paid it no more mind and went about my business.

When I pulled up to my house I noticed one of my horse trailers was gone. My wife, Shelly, told me James Marks, a friend who helps our local search-and-rescue team, had borrowed it.

"A lady's been lost up in the mountains in the Eagle Lake area for several days," she said. "There's a bunch of folks out searching for her."

A picture flashed across my mind. I saw a mountain with a high peak that dipped down and then went slightly up again like a camel's hump. Over the area I saw a hand pointing straight at the mountaintop.

I spoke out strongly. "I know where that lady is," I said.

"What? Randy, how do you know?" my wife asked.

"I just had a vision," I said.

Shelly stared at me. After all our years together she knows when I'm joking and when I'm dead serious. She could tell something real important was happening with me, so she stepped back and said, "Okay."

We tried to call the sheriff's office to get more information, but we couldn't get through. Then we switched on the TV. The news was all about the missing lady. Her name was Mildred McGregor; she was sixty-three years old and had been camping with her husband at Indian Springs near Eagle Lake. She had gone off on a hike alone nearly three days earlier, with some water but nothing to eat, and hadn't been seen since. Millie's five children and a whole mess of grandchildren had been alerted—she even had a great-grandchild—and search parties were out looking for her, on foot and horseback, using dogs and helicopters.

I got out a map and gave it a quick scan. "That's where she is," I said, and put my finger right on the spot—Red Mountain. A mountain with a real high peak that dipped down and then went slightly up again like a camel's hump.

"So what are you going to do?" Shelly asked.

Truthfully, I wasn't sure. I'm not one to go venturing off when I don't know much. What if it was my mind playing tricks? The last thing I wanted was to have people say Randy Spears had sent them on a wild-goose chase.

But the more I thought about it the more clearly I saw the image of that hand pointing to the top of Red Mountain. It was as if God himself were telling me to find that lady. I felt drawn into a spiritual presence you just don't mess with, and Shelly felt it too.

"I'm going to call Frank Smith," I told Shelly. "He'll go with me." A local rancher and friend, Frank and I went packing and hunting together.

This part was strange too: After I told Frank about my vision he didn't laugh or act like I was crazy for calling him so late at night. All he said was, "I've been bucking and baling hay all day, Randy. Just give me an hour to rest."

I figured when I found the lady she would need something to eat. Shelly had just made some homemade bread, so she put together some peanut-butter-and-jelly sandwiches and we filled a thermos.

Horses can get skittery and slip on shale and mountain rocks, so I loaded my trailer with two of my most surefooted mules: Barney was for me, and a black one named Fresno Floyd was for the lady (I was *that* sure we'd find her). Our dog, Misty, who was always ready for adventure, jumped in too.

By the time I drove up to Frank's place it was about one in the morning. Frank loaded his best mule, Elvis, and his dog, Garfield. Then we drove off for the Indian Springs campground, where the search party was headquartered. In about an hour we pulled onto the road leading to it, but it was blocked off, I guess to keep the curious away.

I couldn't see a thing in the darkness. But Red Mountain was directly to the north, and I knew Millie McGregor was on it somewhere. We pulled off the road, unloaded the mules and picketed them, and then threw our bedrolls on the ground. It must have been around four in the morning. Frank was soon sawing logs, but I couldn't sleep. I sat there thinking about that poor woman, how cold she must be up there in the dark.

As dawn lightened the peaks around us, I nudged Frank awake. We saddled Barney and Elvis and, leading Fresno Floyd, we rode to the search-party command post. Maybe a hundred searchers were lining up for a morning meeting, and they stared at us as we trotted in, probably wondering who these jokers were.

James Marks, who had borrowed my horse trailer and was part of the mounted search party, was there. I told him about my vision. James took it real straight, said they had already checked Red Mountain, but wished us well and said he would tell the others where we were going.

Frank and I filled our thermoses with coffee and took off. I was sure some of the guys who watched us ride by thought we were out of our minds, but I didn't care. I felt God had given us the job of finding the lost lady.

Under a brilliant blue sky we started up Red Mountain, on an old trail that had already been searched pretty well. I let the mules plod on; I figured I would know where to go when the time was right. About three quarters of the way up, something made me turn Barney off the trail. Fresno Floyd followed along behind.

Frank, on Elvis, went in another direction and I found myself heading up some really rough terrain, over loose rocks. But Barney and Fresno Floyd were surefooted and on we climbed.

As we neared the peak we reached a treacherous spot and came to a halt. Both the mules and Misty wanted to head in another direction; I guess they had had it with the shale and the drop-offs. But I felt we should go upward and to the south, and I figured the One who had put that vision in my mind was leading me. I said to myself, "We'll go to the top of this peak and I'll look down over the edge in case she fell."

We worked our way through a clump of pines and started up another incline. I grabbed Barney's reins and let out a long breath. As sure as I was about my vision, I still couldn't quite believe my eyes. Making her way over the rise toward us was a white-haired lady with a cane.

"*Yaa-hoo!*" I hollered. "Are you the lady who's lost?"

"I'm *not* lost!" she yelled. "I just can't get down from here!"

Sure enough, it was Millie McGregor, in a big straw hat, T-shirt and slacks, with a sweatshirt tied around her waist. We sure were glad to see each other, and Misty ran right up and barked her a greeting. Millie started talking so fast I couldn't get a word in edgewise. She never slowed down, telling me how she had stuffed pine needles into her clothes to keep warm. She said she could see people and dogs searching for her and saw the helicopters overhead. She yelled and waved, but nobody saw her. Her mind was a muddle. She didn't know what to do except pray. She remembered doing a particularly heavy dose of praying about four o'clock that Wednesday afternoon, just about the time I had my first stirrings that someone was in trouble up on Red Mountain.

Millie's trousers were worn away from where she had tried to slide down the rocks on the seat of her pants. She was dehydrated, and mighty glad to get a drink and one of Shelly's peanut-butter-and-jelly sandwiches.

I fired my gun to signal Frank. Then I put Millie on Fresno Floyd and we started down the mountain. Frank and Garfield joined up.

When we rode into the campground, Millie's husband, children and grandchildren were all gathered there. But since we rode in without much fuss or fanfare, and there were so many people wandering around, nobody noticed us coming. When Millie spoke up and said, "Well, I'm back," everybody flipped. A lot of newspaper and TV people came crowding around. I'm not one for cameras, so I helped Millie down from Fresno Floyd and rode off. I told Frank I thought we deserved a fishing trip.

After a night in the hospital Millie was fine. As I see it, she wasn't the only one who got rescued. I had gotten a big boost too, since God could have picked anyone to find that lady, but he chose me. And that has given me a lot of faith to go on. Why worry about the future when there's something bigger out there to help show you the way?

RUN!

Vidal Davila Jr.

There are few natural disasters more powerful and terrifying than a raging forest fire. As a trained wildland firefighter, I frequently work with a Pulaski, a picklike tool with an ax at one end and a small hoe at the other for digging firebreaks, trenches used to slow a fire and keep it from spreading. But I also have another tool, even more basic than my Pulaski, that I take with me into dangerous situations. In August 1988 it saved my life.

My crew had been flown to the Bridger-Teton Wilderness Area in Wyoming to help fight one of the biggest blazes on record. I was just a few thousand feet from an incandescent wall of flame that was eating its way through three-story-high pines and firs. The heavens glowed orange in the smoky night as our twenty-one-man crew frantically dug a firebreak. What many people don't realize is how fast a forest fire moves, and the deafening roar that accompanies it.

It was time to evacuate. The fire was torching—balls of flame leaping from treetop to treetop ahead of the main blaze—a cannonade of exploding pine sap heralding this moving hell. Sizzling debris rained down as we scrambled cross-country. At about 3:00 AM we reached a safe clearing where we caught some sleep.

By 5:30 AM we were awake. I squatted on the ground, hurriedly eating emergency rations. But soon we were back at work, digging frantically. The fire had pursued us.

All day I dug with my Pulaski. I was black with soot. Sweat poured down my face and neck from beneath my safety helmet. Heat seared my lungs as I chopped the stony earth and fought for breath. I was dead on my feet, disoriented by the uncanny noon light funneling through black clouds of smoke. "Lord," I gasped, "keep me safe and alive."

Huge lodgepole pines exploded as the devouring fire advanced. It was nearly on top of us. I swung my Pulaski faster, blinded by sweat. Then I heard a distinct, instructive voice. It was not a shout but a calm, firm command that I managed to hear clearly above the cacophony of the blaze: *Run!*

Instinctively, I hurled aside my Pulaski and sprinted up a small ridge, my feet flying. When I stopped to look back I saw that a tremendous flaming fir had crashed down on the spot where I had been working. I ran back down, found my Pulaski and joined the others smothering the burning giant with dirt.

Our crew boss ran over to me. "You okay?" he asked, staring.

"Sure," I answered, returning to my digging.

"I've never seen anyone react so fast. You must have eyes in the back of your head," he said.

Not in the back of my head. The extra set of eyes I had that fiery day in Wyoming belonged to my guardian angel, the one indispensable thing I have with me always.

Veteran Advice

Glen Brodie

Old-timer. That's who I saw standing on the pitching mound when I went up to bat in our northern Alabama independent baseball league. I would show this old guy a thing or two.

Minutes later I was back in the dugout. He'd struck me out! Four times that Sunday afternoon I went to bat. Four times I struck out. I sulked in the dugout after the game. How could I go 0 for 4 against an old pitcher who threw junk?

"How old are you, son?" It was the pitcher.

I mumbled, "Sixteen."

"I was in the major leagues by about your age," he said. "Injuries cut my career short."

"You did okay today," I said.

"Your mistakes made me look better than I really am." He took me back to the plate and corrected my stance. "Don't try to hit 'em all out of the park." He gave me tips, not only on baseball. "Respect other players and their abilities," he said. "A strong character will gain you more respect than cockiness."

"Thank you, Mister," I said half an hour later. "Thanks a whole lot." He'd made me a new ballplayer. I could feel it.

When next we played his team I looked forward to showing him how I'd taken his advice to heart. But the old-timer wasn't there. I asked one of his teammates where he was.

"Never seen him before that day," he said. "Never seen him since."

Following the Wind

Tom Mylott

On September 11, 2001, I was on the phone at my desk in 2 Chase Manhattan Plaza, a few blocks away from the World Trade Center. The second plane had hit. I was frantically trying to warn people in the downtown buildings I supervised. "We gotta get out of here," my buddy Andre said. "The Towers are collapsing!"

We made our way to the lobby, where blackness enveloped us. People were screaming. "Where do we go?" someone cried.

"Here," I called out, and Andre and I led a few others into the terrifying dark cloud of smoke and dust outside our door. "Follow my voice," I told the group. "We'll head for the East River." The narrow streets of downtown New York are like a maze. How would we find our way in the darkness? *Lord, lead me to the water.* A warm wind pushed me from behind. "This way," I said, suddenly sure, as if a hand were on my back pushing me in the right direction. I plowed ahead, around corners, down steps, through back alleys, calling out every move aloud, until the wind at my back ceased.

Just a little more, Lord. We can't make it without you.
"Are we lost?" someone called.

And then a cool whisper, the familiar breeze that came off the river, hit my face. Once again, I followed the wind until I turned a corner and saw the glittering East River there before me like a promise.

How I Learned to Listen

Ken Hall

Listening wasn't my strong suit as a young man. I drifted in and out of relationships, from job to job, and in and out of graduate school. Nothing ever seemed worth paying attention to for long. One spring day waiting to cross a street I heard a voice in my head: *Cross now!*

But the light's still green, I thought. *Cross now!* the voice said again. I did. The second I stepped onto the curb a sedan barreled through the intersection and smashed into a building right where I had been standing. The driver's brakes had given out. He was okay, but I could have been killed if I'd stayed where I was. For once I'd listened.

I dropped out of school a few weeks later and took a job as a computer programmer. My first week, I went to the printer room. A pretty redhead came in. Her name tag said Jeanette. I turned around to take my printout. *This is the woman you're going to marry.* I hadn't heard that mysterious voice since it saved my life. When I turned back, the woman had gone.

It took me three weeks to track her down. I took a deep breath and knocked on the door to her office. "Hi," I said. "I'm Ken."

I quit changing jobs, married Jeanette and raised a family. I haven't heard the mysterious voice since, but if it comes back, I'll be listening.

The Rabbi and the Dean

Louis Hill

For the third time in the last half hour, I picked up my office phone to make a call and then replaced the receiver without dialing. An ad in *The Chronicle of Higher Education* had caught my eye, and even though I wasn't looking for a new job, the listing had intrigued me. *But I'm perfectly happy where I am*, I told myself. For twenty years I had been teaching civil engineering at Arizona State University, and was now head of the department. Why would I want to move?

The internal prompting—or my own curiosity—wouldn't go away. Something about the way the writer of the ad described his colleagues and campus appealed to me. Finally I dialed the number and Sandy Groesburg introduced himself. An engineering professor, he headed the committee looking for a new dean at his school, a private university in Philadelphia. I took to him immediately. He was thoughtful, intelligent and warm. We talked at length, and before he hung up, he promised to send me an application.

At home that evening I told my wife, Jeanne. She was dumbstruck. "You called a school about a new job?" she asked incredulously.

"It surprised me too," I said sheepishly. When we had originally moved, leaving close friends and our families behind, it was only after much discussion and prayer. We had sat on our back porch steps for hours and discussed the pros and cons of my three teaching offers, deciding that Arizona was where God meant us to be. I felt guilty about challenging God's will and going against my wife's wishes.

"I love where we live," Jeanne said. "I love our church and our friends. I think it would be a mistake to leave."

"Don't worry," I said. "There must be hundreds of applicants for the job probably much better qualified than I am. We'll never have to decide whether to stay or go."

Since Professor Groesburg had been kind enough to send the forms, I felt obligated to fill them out—with fewer qualms now that I had let Jeanne know. But several weeks later Professor Groesburg sent a letter asking me to come to Philadelphia for an interview. "Bring your wife," he wrote. I cringed. *What have I got us into?* I didn't want to move. I didn't want the position. And yet somehow I felt I had to continue pursuing it.

Jeanne was not pleased. "I thought you said there wasn't a chance," she sputtered.

"I thought there wasn't," I said. "I'm as bewildered as you are, but I think we should go. Who knows? Maybe we'll learn something."

She didn't talk much on the long plane ride. When we flew over Pennsylvania, her interest was piqued by the vast stretches of dark green forest and farmland below, so different from Arizona's desert brown. "The city looks lovely," she said after we landed and drove along the leafy streets to the ivy-covered buildings on campus.

A real trouper, she sat by my side all afternoon in the conference room while I was interviewed by the faculty committee. That evening at dinner with the school's president and his wife, Jeanne was her usual convivial self, full of animated conversation about the friendly staff and the handsome campus. By the time we were driven back to the hotel she didn't seem upset anymore.

But I was. Long after she was asleep, I lay awake, troubled. Even though the interview had gone well, I still didn't feel I was the right match for this school. My interests were different; my background dissimilar. I enjoyed bringing industry and academia together, and there seemed little opportunity for that at this school. "What am I doing here?" I asked God. In the silence of the hotel room I listened for an answer. And as I prayed, I sensed that I would know soon. Reassured, I turned out the light and went to sleep.

The next day Sandy Groesburg came to pick us up and show us more of the campus. He led us on a whirlwind tour. We tromped through the gym, into classrooms and deep into the stacks of the library. We explored the faculty club and the offices, and met many professors, but throughout, I remained most impressed by Sandy himself. His thoughtfulness and enthusiasm attracted me.

At day's end, when we sat down for dinner at a restaurant in town, our conversation turned to religion. He was a devout Jew and I a practicing Christian, but we discovered we both were concerned about finding God's will for our lives.

"That's why we'd have a hard time leaving Arizona," I admitted. "When we moved there we knew it was meant to be."

Sandy's eyebrows shot up. "You see God's will as a destination?" he asked.

"Yes. How do you see it?"

He hesitated for a moment. "I think it is more the path we follow than the goal." He rubbed his chin thoughtfully, and then put his hands back in the pockets of his tweed jacket. "In fact, I think there can be a number of destinations on our lifelong journey. God shows us what they are as we follow him.

"At any rate," Sandy added, "I really appreciate the time we've had together. You've helped me make a big decision." Jeanne and I nodded, not knowing what he was referring to, but too polite to ask.

The next morning on our flight home we both started talking at once. Jeanne apologized for giving me a hard time about the trip. "Professor Groesburg was right. It had never occurred to me that the Lord might want us somewhere else now, though he wanted us in Arizona before."

I laughed. "You don't need to worry about moving to Philadelphia. I don't want the job there. But now I know why I made the trip: Sandy got me thinking. Maybe there's a dean's job somewhere else that might be right for me."

Back home I began to read the education classifieds and study the notices posted on the department bulletin board, pursuing different opportunities. After much rumination and prayer, I ended up taking a position as dean of engineering at the University of Akron. It turned out to be just the right place, full of exciting challenges. Of course, one of the first things I did was to call my friend Sandy Groesburg. I wanted to thank him for his good advice.

"I'm sorry," the secretary told me. "Dr. Groesburg is no longer here. He's studying to become a rabbi."

I smiled to myself, thinking back on the conversations Sandy and I had had about faith and education and serving God. *So that's what he meant when he told me I had helped clarify a decision he was making.* He had found a new destination.

Since then Jeanne and I have made several more big moves, including a return to Arizona. Each time I've thought of Sandy Groesburg. He showed me that God's will takes us on a never-ending journey.

· 5 ·

ℋONORING ℳEMORY

WHAT IS OUR HOPE, OR JOY, OR CROWN OF
REJOICING? IS IT NOT EVEN YOU IN THE PRESENCE
OF OUR LORD JESUS CHRIST AT HIS COMING?
—*1 Thessalonians 2:19*

*Lord, I thank you that, even in our grief, you can give
grace-filled reminders of our departed loved ones that
honor their memory—and you.*

READY TO WEAR

Sally Whittington

"This plant belongs in the composter," I muttered to myself, shaking my head as I surveyed what was left of my latest attempt to grow a gardenia—nothing but mottled yellow leaves and shriveled brown buds that hung limply off the brittle branches. Heaven knows, I had tried everything my mother taught me about caring for houseplants—more light, less water, spraying, fertilizing, repotting, even prayer—but nothing seemed to work.

I wish Mama were here now, I thought. Mother's Day was coming up, the second one since her death, and the pain of losing her was still so fresh.

There is a Mother's Day tradition I follow of wearing a red flower if one's mother is alive and a white one if she is not. I had hoped that cultivating a white gardenia, Mama's favorite flower, would help me through the grief of her passing.

Mama had a way with all things green. My sister and I always joked, "Mama could make a telephone pole sprout leaves and bear fruit."

Why can't I? I thought. Still, I couldn't bear to throw the dead plant away. Instead, I stuffed it into a dark corner of our bathroom. I didn't water it, didn't prune it. I just left it there until I could deal with it.

My husband had asked me if I was going to wear a white corsage to church that Mother's Day. *And wear my grief like a badge for all to see?*

"No," I told him. "I know it's been over a year, but I'm just not ready yet." *And I don't know if I'll ever be ready,* I added silently.

Sunday morning I woke up early to get dressed and made up for church. Still groggy, I walked to the bathroom. Suddenly I was jolted awake by a pleasant scent. *Did someone spray air freshener in there?* I wondered. I pushed the door open and stepped into the bathroom.

That morning I knew I would be ready to wear a white corsage for Mama. In that dark corner, bright as if it had a light of its own, bloomed a perfect white gardenia.

JUST FOR DADDY

Kathy Schendle

I missed Daddy something awful. I couldn't go into the kitchen without thinking of him. He was the cook in our family, always trying out new recipes and methods. Once he rigged up a big metal fish fryer so he could fry catfish over a fire pit in our yard.

Then he took sick. That was the only time I ever came up with a recipe for him.

He'd come down with cancer and lost his appetite. Our family doctor made house calls just to plead with him to eat. I tried too. "Please eat *something*, Daddy," I said one day, stroking his hand. "You need to keep your weight on."

"I'd love to have some pecan pie," he finally said with a mischievous glint in his sunken blue eyes. Pecan pie. His favorite. But it was made mostly of butter, nuts and corn syrup. The doctor thought it was too rich. I had to whip up something just as good that would be good for Daddy too. I messed around with a few recipes and, after some trial and error, baked a batch of pecan-pie muffins. I thought they were delicious. But would Daddy? You bet he did. He was crazy for them. Even when he didn't feel like having any he'd wrap one up and put it in a drawer, "just in case."

Pretty soon his visitors wanted muffins too. Even his nurse, Winnie. "Sorry," he'd tease, "but my daughter made them just for me." It was the one thing I could do for him while doctors, chemo and everything else did its best. It was our special bond through a very hard time.

Daddy died in August 2003. I quit making the muffins. It was too painful. Then one morning Winnie called. "I was thinking of your daddy and those pecan muffins. Think you could make a batch for me?" It was the least I could do for the woman who'd taken such good care of my father. I chopped up the pecans and added the other ingredients, tears rolling down my cheeks. *Lord,* I said, *I miss Daddy. Help me with my grief.*

Six muffins. I wrapped them in a towel and put them into a basket to take to Winnie. I cried and laughed on my way over, remembering how Daddy would hoard them all. I pulled up to Winnie's and checked the muffins again. I counted them . . . and counted them again. There were only five muffins! They'd never left my sight, yet somehow one was missing.

Daddy might have been gone, but at that moment I could feel him close to me. Like the warm lingering smell of a fresh-baked muffin.

CHOW BY HER SIDE

Marjory Wilson

My sister, Linda, was the bravest person I knew. When she lost her sight to diabetes she had to give up teaching. She could no longer read the books she loved. But she remained independent, facing each day with joy. Even death was no match for Linda. "I'm just making a transition," she explained to me after doctors told her she didn't have much time left. "In heaven I'll have my sight back—I can read all the time!"

Only one thing worried Linda about leaving this world: her dog, Sam. The big black chow was her constant companion. Linda's husband, James, and son, Will, understood what was happening. But could Sam?

Days after the funeral, Will returned to college, and Sam searched the house in vain for his beloved owner. Then one day he disappeared. No one in our small town could find him anywhere. "I have some bad news," James said over the phone to Will. "It's about Sam."

"I already know," Will cut in. "In a dream I saw Mom reading in a beautiful library. Sam was at her feet. He's not coming back, Dad. He's with Mom."

We never saw Sam again. But I know he's where he belongs. He didn't disappear. He just made a transition.

$\mathcal{S}$OME SPECIAL MAGIC?

German Martinez

$\mathcal{P}$urple crape myrtles were Momma's favorite. I turned into the driveway and stared at the spot out front where she'd wanted me to put a tree. "One day," I always told her, but I never got around to it before she died. A good son keeps his promises to his momma.

I got out of my car. A young man was trimming the hedge next door. "Wow!" I said. "Nice work. I've been thinking about doing some planting over here. You know anything about crape myrtles?"

"Expensive tree," he said, "and hard to come by this time of year."

I explained why I hated to put it off any longer. "It's never too late to honor a mother's wish," he said.

Feeling like a weight had been lifted from my chest, I went inside. Somehow I knew that gardener would come through for me.

I pulled up to my house a couple days later. Something was different. I opened the car door and got out. Nothing had been changed, but the lawn looked greener, brighter. The bushes seemed more lush. Had the gardener worked some special magic here in my yard too? He wasn't around for me to ask.

Early next morning I stepped out to get the newspaper. I nearly fell over backward. There, in the very spot Momma had designated, was a beautiful blooming purple crape myrtle. The gardener! It must have been—but when? How could I have overlooked it the night before? My neighbor couldn't shed any light on the mystery. And neither of us ever saw that gardener again.

A Toothpick (or Two?)

Lucille Gearing

If there's one thing I associate with my husband, Phil, it's a toothpick. Every night after dinner he'd go hunting for one. One Christmas, our children, Barbara and Tom, gift-wrapped a box of them for him. He always said it was the best present ever.

When Phil got weaker and weaker from cancer, I set him up in a hospital bed in our room and cared for him at home. After he died I could still see the imprint of the bed wheels in the carpet. I was never so lonely in my life.

A couple of months after Phil died, Barbara called. "The doctor found a suspicious lump. I'm having it checked out tomorrow. Pray for me."

Pray I did. All night long. *How I wish Phil were here,* I thought before I dozed off at dawn. I climbed out of bed a short time later. My eye caught something white on the rug. A toothpick, stuck into the nap, right by the spot where Phil's bed used to be. *How could I have missed it before?* I vacuumed to keep busy till Barbara called. "False alarm!" she said. "I'm fine!"

That night I fell asleep with a prayer on my lips. *Thank you, God, and tell Phil I love him.* When I woke up there was another toothpick in the carpet. I could never have missed two of them. God definitely wanted me to know he was watching over our family, on earth and in heaven.

Incidentally, Phil died at age eighty-two with a full set of teeth—the toothpicks must have helped!

Wrong Train?

Dorothy Lilja Harrison

I stood with my family at the train station, but my mind was on my last visit with my dying father. The funeral service that summer morning was somewhat of a comfort, but memories of the vital person my father had once been kept competing with that of a shriveled old man in a nursing home. *Just where and how was he now?* I wondered.

The train arrived to take our son back to his camp counselor's job. We all hugged him good-bye, and he mounted the steps into the car that had stopped in front of us. Hoping for a glimpse of Jeff and another wave, I stood on tiptoe and scanned the windows. A man smiled down at me. He looked exactly like my father. The man was impeccably dressed and even had a familiar twinkle in his eye. That used to mean Daddy was tickled about something.

I nudged my husband. "Doesn't that man look just like my father?" He agreed, as did the children.

Just before the train lurched forward on the tracks, Jeff jumped back off. "Wrong train!" he called to us. Jeff had double-checked and this train wasn't even on the schedule.

Wrong train? Not for me. Now I knew for certain that my dad was well and happy and ready for a new journey. I believe it was God's amazing consolation for a grieving daughter.

HEAVEN'S TRAIL

Mary Louise Hillyard

*B*roken sunlight filtered through the ceiling of branches high above our campsite near the Eel River in Humboldt County, California. I worked at the camp stove cooking dinner for my husband, Arland, and our teenage girls, Maureen and Cheryl. Some potatoes I'd boiled that morning sizzled in a big cast-iron pan. Roasting alongside were hot dogs and a batch of squash we'd picked up earlier at a vegetable stand on the Avenue of the Giants, the famous scenic road that runs through a stretch of particularly huge California redwoods. "Warmed-over potatoes," Dad called them, back when he cooked up meals for my brother, sisters, Mom, and me on the camping trips we took as children.

The woods always made me think of Dad—but this summer that was especially so. It was almost a year to the day since he'd suffered a severe stroke, transforming him from the vital, energetic person I'd known all my life into someone who could no longer do anything for himself. He was in a nursing home in Erie, Pennsylvania, just down the road from my brother, Bud. "Dad doesn't even know me anymore," Bud had said before we left on our trip. I wondered if we should go cross-country instead.

"You're doing the right thing," Bud told me. "You know how much Dad loved taking us to the woods when we were kids. He wouldn't want the girls to be stuck in some hospital. He'd want them to be sitting around a campfire and walking trails, the way we used to with him."

Dad always made sure we were the first campers out in the spring and the last ones to leave in the fall. No one loved nature more than he did. I promised Bud we would phone every couple of days.

I pushed the food around the pan with a long spatula, feeling a rush of second thoughts. The last time I'd checked in, Dad's condition had been stable. *God, I hope I did the right thing coming out here.* I felt someone behind me. Dad? I turned around. Nothing there but the massive, silent trunks of the redwoods.

"Arland, Maureen, Cheryl!" I called. "Supper's ready."

Arland and the girls came running. Dishing out the food, I looked up and noticed a forest ranger coming toward our campsite, clipboard in hand.

"Good evening," I said. "Would you like some dinner?"

"No thanks, ma'am," the ranger said. He removed his hat and sat at our picnic table. "I'm doing a little research for a field report. Would you mind if I joined you?"

The ranger asked us a few questions—where we were from, how long we were staying—while we ate. "We love this area," I said. "The trails are gorgeous."

"We have a brand-new one, on the Avenue of the Giants. You won't find it on the maps yet, but it's magical." The forest ranger gave us directions. The trail was right across from the vegetable stand we'd stopped by earlier. The ranger stood up, put his hat back on, and bobbed his head good-bye. "It was real nice talking to you folks." Campers were set up here and there among the trees around us. I was surprised that he didn't stop to talk to any of them for his field report. Just us.

After dinner we drove to a pay phone. I could immediately hear in Bud's voice that something was wrong.

"Mary Louise, Dad's gone. He passed away just after I talked to you last. The funeral was this morning. I've had the highway patrol trying to find you. I'm sorry."

Back at the campsite we spent the rest of the evening gathered around the fire, sharing memories of Dad and crying. I told the girls how much I'd loved being in the woods with him when I was their age—how he was always ready to scout out a new trail or find a perfect fishing spot no one else knew about.

Finally, we all went to bed. But I couldn't sleep. *Lord, I should have been there to tell Dad good-bye.*

"Let's go on one more walk before we head home," I said to Arland the next morning. "For Dad." We got on the Avenue of the Giants and drove to the vegetable stand.

There was the new trail, just as the ranger had said. I was surprised we hadn't noticed it before. The trailhead was clearly marked. We got out and set off into the woods.

Delicate flowers and ferns sprang from the forest floor. Redwood trunks rose like columns up to the leafy canopy, where birds flitted, their faraway calls the only sounds in the woods. This really was another world.

Deeper and deeper into the forest we walked, the girls in front, Arland and I holding hands behind them. We came to a spot where a redwood trunk lay across the path, illuminated by a single ray of light. "You and the girls go on," I said to Arland. "I want to sit a while."

Arland touched my cheek. "We'll see you on the way back."

The three of them disappeared down the path. I sat in the circle of light and ran my hand along the rough bark. *Dad, I'm sorry I wasn't there with you. But you know how much I love you, how much I always will.* The sun wrapped me in warmth and held me. I looked up into the blinding light and listened in the perfect silence.

"Good-bye, Dad."

Arland and the girls got back and joined me on the log. My sadness was still there, but something was different. In some strange way, I felt it was okay I hadn't been there with Dad after all.

We walked along the peaceful path out to the edge of the forest. "It's hard to step back into the real world," I said at the trail opening.

By that afternoon we were packed up and on our way home. Again and again in the weeks that followed, when Dad came to mind, I'd immediately think of that spot in the woods. I liked to imagine Dad full of his old enthusiasm as he explored heaven's trails.

When Arland's vacation rolled around the next year we went back to the Eel River. "Let's go to the special trail," the girls said on our first morning there. I couldn't wait to see it again.

We got on the Avenue of Giants, and slowed down at the vegetable stand. "This is the place, but where's the trail?" Arland said. Across from the stand there was no sign of a trail entrance. We got out of the car and looked around. The underbrush was so thick you could hardly even step into the woods. We asked at the vegetable stand.

"Trail?" the man said. "There's no trail over there. Never has been."

We drove up and down the road, looking for some sign of a trail entrance. Finally, we stopped by the ranger station. When the guys on duty didn't know of any such trail, we described the ranger we'd met.

"I'm sorry, ma'am," one of them said. "We know every ranger in the area. We don't know who you're talking about. And there is *no such trail*."

Arland and the girls looked as confused as the rangers did. But I wasn't. We had walked on a heavenly trail, and Dad had heard my good-bye.

$\mathcal{A}$ Vase for Mom

Rhonda Lowther

$\mathcal{M}$om's red vase sits in my curio cabinet, and sometimes the sunlight hits it just the way it did the day I first saw it. I was eight and visiting my grandparents for the weekend. I cleaned my plate at Friday dinner. Granddaddy pressed a quarter into my hand as a reward.

Oh, the things I could buy with that quarter! Pixy Stix, little wax Coke bottles, the tiny dot candies on paper. Saturday morning we headed for the little grocery store at the strip mall across the street. We were about to go inside when my eye caught a flash of red in the window of a secondhand store. Red like the lamps in our living room and the stemware glasses and candleholders my mom used for special occasions. *Mom's red,* I thought, suddenly excited. *I have to get it for her.*

"Can I look in this store?" I asked Granddaddy.

"Sure, Rhonda. I'll be in the grocery."

I slipped inside the shop. "Howdy, young lady," the man behind the cash register said. I put my quarter on the glass-top counter.

"I'd like that red vase in the window," I said.

The man smiled and shook his head. "I'm afraid it'll take more than that."

I stared at the red vase, afraid to ask the price of a treasure like that, then slunk out of the store. That night Granddaddy and Nannie watched *Lawrence Welk* on TV. I sat on the couch between them, dreaming of the red vase that I knew Mom would love. I saved my allowance, returned bottles for pennies and put aside every cent I could. Next time I visited my grandparents, my pink, beaded purse was so heavy I was afraid the handle would break. Again Granddaddy gave me a quarter for cleaning my plate. The next morning I marched into the second-hand shop. The red vase was still there!

I dumped all the coins on the counter. "Is this enough?"

The man looked at me and looked at the dimes, quarters, nickels and pennies—mostly pennies. Finally he nodded. "It's just the right amount," he said.

Mom loved the vase. She put it into her china cabinet and took it out for special occasions. Later, she moved in with my husband and me, and the vase came with her. Then she got the cancer diagnosis.

She fought a valiant battle. I put the vase with flowers in it by her bedside to cheer her up. Or I put it on the table if she felt strong enough to join us at mealtime. Then one awful day she was gone. The vase went back into the cabinet. I didn't want to look at it. It made me miss Mom too much. *How will I face life without her?* I asked in my prayers.

One day a friend was visiting. An antiques dealer. I caught him admiring the vase. "It belonged to my mother," I said.

"May I?" He picked it up. "I haven't seen something like this in years. It's a special glass, a technique that's rarely done anymore. It's called ruby glass."

I felt my breath go. For one brief moment I was back at the strip mall, staring into the secondhand store and seeing the vase for the first time. And feeling the wonderment of a divine hand. For you see, my mother's name was Ruby.

Martita's Door

Lisa Diaz

Rows of mourners filled the ancient wooden pews of the centuries-old church, so different from the modern churches I was used to in America. Everything about Antigua, Guatemala, was different and beautiful to me: majestic cathedrals, cobblestone streets and distant volcanoes. I only wished I were visiting for a happier reason. My husband, Oscar, and I had flown back to his home to attend his mother's funeral—on my first visit. I mourned for Oscar's loss and for myself as well. How I wished I had been able to get to know Martita Diaz, my mother-in-law.

I struggled to follow the priest's eulogy in Spanish. I could well imagine what he might be saying. I had heard so many stories about Martita since I'd met Oscar, about how she seemed to be like a mother to everyone she met.

Oscar told me he often came home from school and found her chatting with a stranger. When he asked who the person was, his mother said, "Just someone who needed someone to talk to." He described her cooking in her tiny kitchen, boiling giant pots on the stove—pots she could hardly lift on her own. She wasn't cooking just for her family, but for anyone who might be hungry and had no money for food themselves. Word got around about the kind lady who fed the poor, and Martita's church listed her house as an official soup kitchen.

If Martita made such an impression on me, I thought, looking around at the others gathered in her memory, *what must she have meant to the people she saw every day here in Antigua?*

I heard footsteps in the center aisle and turned to look. A scruffy golden-brown dog trotted into the church. *How did that dog get in here?* I love animals, but the church was God's house and a dog did not belong in it. Someone would have to shoo the animal out.

Without fanfare, the dog walked right up to the altar and sat down as if she were a noble guard. No one made a move. I turned my attention back to the priest, but found it hard to concentrate. My eyes kept wandering back to that silly animal, sitting so proudly by the coffin. As if she had some purpose here. *Don't be ridiculous,* I thought. *She's just wandered in where she doesn't belong.*

I hoped no one else was distracted. Such a shame for something like this to happen during Martita's funeral. For all my mother-in-law had done for others, she deserved a respectful service. Now this annoying dog had ruined it.

At the end of the service, we all rose to follow Martita's coffin in a procession to the cemetery at the bottom of the hill. The dog got up too and led the way down the aisle.

"Why doesn't someone tie that animal up?" I whispered to Oscar.

"She's not bothering anyone," Oscar said with a shrug.

We walked out to the cobblestone road that led to the cemetery. I got into a car with my husband behind the hearse. The other mourners followed on foot. As we drove slowly down the road I looked out the back window. The golden-haired dog trotted right behind us. The other mourners were supposed to be following our car, but it looked more like they were following the golden dog right through the big iron gates.

At the burial site we gathered around the mausoleum and watched as the coffin was placed inside. Oscar read a tribute he had written for his mother. *"Las puertas de mi madre,"* he said, *"siempre estaban abiertas para quienes necesitaban ayuda."* My mother's door was always open to those in need.

The dog sat in front, listening, it seemed, to every word Oscar said.

When Oscar finished, the mourners filed back out of the cemetery. The golden dog sat by the mausoleum until they had all gone. Then she turned and with slow, deliberate steps, walked out of the cemetery's iron gates.

Only the family and the priest were left behind. His eyes followed the dog walking beyond the gates. "The dog has never come into the church before," he said.

"So why would she come to a funeral?" I wondered.

"She is a street dog," the priest explained. "She has no home, no one to belong to. But there was one place she was always welcome. Martita fed her every day, just as she fed the others who needed her help."

I looked back at the golden dog, now making her way up the cobblestone street. I had thought she had no place at a church service. But everyone—strays of any kind— had a place in God's house. He turned no one away. Martita had lived her life following God's example. What better place than at her funeral for me to learn to follow hers?

Amanda's Gifts

Edie Blanchard

If I were asked to choose one word to describe my granddaughter Amanda, I would say it without hesitation: "Alive." This is how I will always think of her. Soon after her birth in 1997, I said to my husband, "You can see both the past and the future in her eyes." Benny nodded in agreement, even though it was a strange thing to say. To a newborn child the past meant being with God and his angels. Little did I know then that Amanda's future would be in heaven too, in only four short years. And I didn't know how unprepared I would be, though I had twenty years of experience in hospice counseling. I was no stranger to death, and my faith was strong. But Amanda was unique in my life. She was a gift I didn't want to give back.

Our daughter, Ceci, and her husband, Brad, never imagined Amanda had any health problems. She had boundless energy, and her smile could light up a room like our Las Vegas sunshine. Then she got pneumonia her first Christmas, and had a series of tests. The diagnosis was heartbreaking. Amanda had cystic fibrosis, a genetic disorder that affects the body's vital functions, including breathing and digestion. The doctor told us that thousands of children are diagnosed with CF every year, but for us—her parents and grandparents and her eight-year-old sister, Alisha—only one child mattered: Amanda.

Her disease demanded constant attention, and her dad learned how to give her treatments at home. Amanda never complained. She had more important things to do. She often visited the elderly couple who lived next door. She liked to shop, and always carried a purse with special treasures inside, like a miniature race car her dad had given her. She loved to play with her grandpa, whom she called PaPa. Benny was her best buddy, and she was the elf in his garden, begging rides in his wagon. "Ring around the rosy," she sang. "PaPa, fall down!" Then she squealed with laughter as he sprawled in the yard.

Amanda's second bout with pneumonia ended in lung surgery when she was two. Just before her fourth birthday, she developed lung infections that never seemed to go away. She climbed on my lap during her birthday party. There was a cloud of pain in her eyes I'd never seen. "I really sick," she said.

Four days later Amanda suffered cardiac arrest during a routine procedure at the hospital. We rushed to be with her. "PaPa's here," Benny said, and Amanda's eyes fluttered open for a second and then closed. All my hospice training seemed to vanish. *God, help me. How can I get through this?*

Amanda succumbed to her illness a few days after her birthday. She was once again with God and his angels, and with their mercy we began to understand that she was still with us. When her dad arrived home from the hospital after her death, their elderly neighbors hurried to see him. They had answered a knock at their door, and saw Amanda on the porch. In their hearts they heard her say, "I love you." An eight-year-old cousin, devastated by Amanda's death, sat with me at her gravesite. I was surprised to see a smile on his face. "Amanda walked here beside me," Trevor said, "and said she loved me."

I wished I could find that peace for myself. *Are the old and young closer to God?* I wondered. *Do they hear his angels more clearly than the rest of us?* One night I was checking my e-mail. I clicked print on my computer. Instead of the letter I expected, out came a page splashed with a bright burst of yellow. Amanda's favorite color! Where had it come from? Then in my heart I heard Amanda whisper, "Don't cry, Gramma Edie. I love you."

A few days after the funeral, Benny came into the house. "I got a message from Amanda," he said quietly. He was in the garden sitting in his wagon, and the wheel broke off. "I heard Amanda laugh, and she said, 'Fall down, PaPa.'"

These experiences were like gifts from my granddaughter, and I shared them with Ceci. She had one for me too. Amanda loved the song "Tomorrow" from the musical *Annie*. The CD had been stuck in the car's player for months. On Ceci's drive home one day, the CD popped out in her hand. "Amanda was telling me she's happy in her own tomorrows," she said.

Eventually Amanda's dad also received a message. No one could find her purse, the special purse she'd always carried with her treasures inside. More than a month after her death, Brad opened his toolbox with the photo of Amanda he'd pasted in the lid. He found a surprise: the miniature race car he'd given her, the one she'd carried in her purse.

We each received a message from Amanda, saying good-bye in ways as unique as she was. I have no doubt that she is happy in heaven with God and his angels. Amanda was an angel in our midst for four short years. She will always be alive in my heart.

HEAVEN'S MUSIC

Janet S. Bennington

Fifty years seems like a long time for two people to be together, but it's not long enough when you're in love. That's how it was for my husband and me. Doc always sang country love songs to me, the ones that were popular back in the 1950s when we were courting. "Have I Told You Lately That I Love You?" was one of our favorites. He sang it to me more times than I can count. His voice grew weak, as did he because of illness, but to me Doc still sounded just like Tex Ritter on our old-time radio.

When we celebrated our golden anniversary, Doc was failing. "I'm thinking about heaven," he said. I wanted him to be at peace, but I didn't know how I'd get along without him and his love songs.

True enough, after he was gone, love seemed far away. Friends tried to be a comfort. One gave me a brand-new radio, but I couldn't bring myself to turn it on. Not without Doc around. Then, one night, I heard music coming from the other bedroom. "Have I told you lately that I love you ..." *How could that radio have turned itself on?* I wondered. But it hadn't. The radio was off, as usual. It was heaven's music I must have heard, country-style. Love was just a song away.

· 6 ·

Answering Prayers

THE EFFECTIVE, FERVENT PRAYER OF A
RIGHTEOUS MAN AVAILS MUCH.

—*James 5:16*

*Lord, sometimes you dramatically answer our
prayers; at other times you respond subtly yet surely.
As we listen, help us discern your ways and means.*

End of the Line

Jodi Panko

I work in a parking garage near the University of Nebraska, so I see it all the time: A driver will pay the parking fee for the car behind him, and then that driver will pay for the next and so on. It's a bit of a tradition, especially at sports events. A random act of kindness that makes people smile.

One night there was a ballet at the campus performing-arts center. A man gave me double the fee and asked that I let the people in the next car know he'd paid for them too. "You're all set," I told the teenagers in the van. Then they paid for the next guy. The chain reached the tenth car. A new record!

Car No. 11 pulled up: a mom driving an old station wagon. She'd won tickets and wanted her daughter to see her first ballet, but didn't have money for parking. I told her the car in front had already paid.

"No kidding! I prayed God would help me with this." In this case, I guess it wasn't such a random act after all.

When Michael Met Rosie

Claire Guthrie

"We're getting a dog! We're getting a dog!" the kids chanted from the back of our car on the way to Pennsylvania to pick up Rosie, our new Lab, from her foster home. I glanced back at my teenager, Aaron; his younger sister, Rachael, seven; and brother Joshua, five, who hadn't stopped talking about Rosie since we'd pulled out of our driveway in Virginia an hour before. Only my two-year-old, Michael, was silent. He was just as excited, but he couldn't join in with the chatter of his siblings. I felt a familiar ache in my chest, knowing how badly Michael wanted to join in, and knowing it was impossible. It was a pain I felt often, ever since we found out about Michael's condition.

I knew something was different about Michael at six months old. Josh and Rachael walked and talked early. But our otherwise healthy-looking baby boy had trouble even crawling; Michael couldn't roll over and he couldn't sit up without toppling. Even more troubling, he never developed baby talk. I wondered if he'd ever speak. His brother Aaron has cerebral palsy, and I feared Michael might have a disability too. In fact, Michael was diagnosed with dyspraxia, a developmental disorder that makes it difficult to perform complex movements. Michael's trouble with speaking was part of that disorder, called childhood apraxia of speech. He wanted to speak, but his mind just wouldn't let him.

Even now, at two years and three months, he still couldn't say much more than "mama" or "dada" when he wanted us for something. And often, we couldn't understand what he wanted. His speech therapist helped us teach him some basic sign language. Even that was hard for him. A few days earlier, Michael tried to ask me for something, but he couldn't form the signs. Instead, he began gesturing wildly. "I'm sorry, Michael. I don't understand," I told him. His face turned a deep shade of red; he went into a tantrum, letting out a high-pitched scream. I felt so helpless. My baby was hurting—and I couldn't do anything for him.

I looked in the rearview mirror back at Michael, who was staring out the window. This dog, I hoped, would be something he could enjoy. My husband, Doug, and I had done our research. We looked for a Labrador, a breed known to be good with kids. A young dog, so it could grow up with our children. We found Rosie on the

Web site for a Lab rescue agency. A fourteen-month-old chocolate Lab, with experience around babies, children and cats. All of our "dream dog" qualities. But would she be right for our family? Was I wrong to hope? Finally we pulled up to Rosie's foster home. I silently prayed, *Please, God, let Rosie be right for our kids...especially Michael, but don't let me hope for too much.*

Doug lifted Michael out of his car seat while I went to the door with the other kids. "You must be here to see Rosie," the woman said. And there Rosie was, standing in the foyer, tongue hanging out, her tail wagging wildly. Aaron, Rachael and Joshua ran up to her. "Rosie, you're so beautiful," Rachael said, ruffling her smooth fur. "Hi, Rosie," said Aaron, scratching her behind the ears. *Love at first sight,* I thought. But what about my two-year-old? Michael ambled over. He patted her gently on the head. Rosie nuzzled against him. I breathed a sigh of relief.

I was about to follow the woman into the other room to talk to her about the dog when I heard a voice, an unfamiliar voice. "Rosie," the voice said, strong and clear. "Rosie!" It was Michael. I looked at Doug, my mouth agape. "Rosie!" he said again, nuzzling against the dog. Now, Doug and I were the speechless ones.

Rosie sat in the back with the kids on the way home. "You're going to love our house, Rosie Pops," I said.

The kids loved the nickname. The whole ride back, that's what we called her. We were about halfway home when Michael spoke again. "Rosie Pops," he said. One word was amazing enough, but two words together? In one day? Doug and I chalked it up to Michael's excitement. *Don't get your hopes up*, I reminded myself. How often had I seen progress when there was none? *God*, I prayed once more, *make this dog a good fit for our family.*

A few days later I was folding laundry, watching the kids play with Rosie. Michael stood next to her, petting her as she rubbed up against him. Then, without warning, she jumped, and Michael lost his balance. I watched in horror as he fell over. I dropped everything and rushed to him. But I calmed down when I saw Michael laughing. He pushed off the carpet and stood, following Rosie again as she raced around the room. I watched more closely. Rosie wasn't being reckless. Every time she nudged Michael, she did it gently, almost as if she were testing him. And each time he fell, she waited by his side, studying him until he rose to his feet. It was a little game they were playing. A game Rosie was using to learn things about Michael.

The next night, at dinner, Michael shocked everyone when he said "juice." Right out of the blue! A day later, he said "dog." It's hard to describe the astonishment that took over our house. Over the next few weeks, he added more words: candy, cookie, car. He was also becoming less clumsy, rarely stumbling. His speech therapist was baffled. "Kids with apraxia don't progress like this," she told me.

I was baffled too. I went on an apraxia Web site and e-mailed for information. "Is there anything about dogs helping kids with apraxia?" I asked. Yes, as it turned out. Studies found the stimulation a dog brings can awaken muscles necessary for speech and other bodily movements. Each time Michael laughed, fell and got back up again, his brain was busily connecting the dots between his muscles and his actions. Now I knew why he was improving.

I went up to tuck Michael into bed. He was exhausted from playing with Rosie all day. I pulled the blanket up to his chest and gave him a kiss. Michael moved his lips. "Luv vu," he said. *Did he say that?* Michael spoke again. "Luv vu," he said.

I wrapped my arms around him. "I love you, Michael," I whispered through my tears. "I love you too." I shut off his light and headed to the living room. Rosie lay curled up by the TV. I stroked behind her ears and told her what a good girl she was. She was teaching Michael so much— and me as well. God answers prayers in many ways. This time he chose a dog to answer ours. Hope comes in many forms, and I must never forsake it.

A Time to Remember

Eleanor M. Behman

All through our twenty-three years of marriage Ron was a loving husband and wonderful father. Though he agreed the kids and I should go to church, he seldom came with us. I hinted; I cajoled. And I prayed, *Please, Lord, open Ron's heart to you.* Ron continued to have mixed feelings about his faith, and I wondered if my prayers had any effect.

When our oldest daughter, Reneé, went into the hospital to deliver our first grandchild I asked Ron to come with us, but he decided to stay at work. I fumed silently. After Reneé gave birth to a beautiful, healthy baby girl, I called Ron. "Hi, Grandpa. Your granddaughter has arrived. You should have been here."

"No," he said. "I had to be here today. I'll explain later. Please find out what time the baby was born. It's important."

I hung up, confused, but I found out the time of birth. When I picked Ron up that evening he handed me a folded piece of paper.

"Don't open it yet, Ellie. Just listen," he began. "A friend came into the shop today and told me about how important Jesus Christ is in our lives. Something he said struck a chord with me. When he asked me to pray with him, I agreed. I can't explain it, but afterward I felt different."

It was the moment I had been waiting for. But instead of being thrilled, I felt hurt. *Twenty-three years I've been pushing for this*, I thought, *and his friend can make him change just like that?*

"There's more," he continued. "I felt compelled to say a prayer for Reneé and her child. Just as I sat down at my desk again, I heard a baby's cry, sharp and clear. I looked around, but there was no one in the shop. Then, for some reason, I checked the time. I wrote it down on that slip.

"You know," Ron continued, "I always asked the Lord, 'If you are truly present, give me a sign, and I will believe.' But it didn't work that way. First I believed, and *then* he let me hear my granddaughter cry."

When I looked at the slip I realized Ron's friend hadn't changed his mind any more than I had. It was an act far beyond either of us, one that had been in the works for twenty-three years. For Ron had written 6:23—the exact time of our granddaughter's birth.

WHO'LL START THE RAIN?

Wanda Rosseland

It's too dry for June 1. For the third year in a row, drought conditions were parching Montana. I could feel the relentless heat on my face and arms as I headed across the farmyard to the house.

Earlier in the spring when we took the cows to grass, instead of new crested wheat greening the hills and creek bottoms, brittle brown stems from last year crunched under the cows' hooves. Normally, snowpack in the mountains fed the rivers through the summer, but now the rivers were nothing more than useless shallow streams.

Inside I spoke to my friend Jeanie on the phone. "What can we do about this drought?" I asked.

"Wanda, you're good with words. Write a prayer to send out. Something to get everyone praying."

I can't do that, I thought. But then I sat down at my computer and began to type: "We need to pray for rain to fall across our state of Montana." The words flowed. "Soft, gentle rain over our mountains, steady, even rain moving across our prairies. Rain soaking deep into the ground. . . . We have no covering for our peaks. Send the snow to mantle their tops." *Snow! That's outrageous. It's June already.* But the words kept coming.

I e-mailed the prayer to family and friends and urged them to e-mail it to others. I don't know how many people prayed that day, but on June 4, I got an e-mail from my sister: "Missoula got six inches of snow." The next message was from a friend in Libby in the northwest corner of Montana: "It's pouring! We've been getting downpours all day!" I rushed outside and looked at the sky. Clouds— heavy gray ones, with rain. One, two, three drops falling ever so gently on my face, each one an answer to prayer.

MIRACLE IN MOZAMBIQUE

Brenda Lange

$\mathcal{P}$eople thought I was a little crazy to start Village of Love in Mozambique. A single woman running an orphanage by herself in a desperately poor, politically unstable country? But something told me this was my life's calling. I had skills as a nurse, and as a result of decades of civil war Mozambique was a country of orphans. I knew my path wouldn't be easy, but I had faith that God would give me the direction and strength necessary to do his work.

My first step was to enroll in a school for missionaries in Africa. There I was trained to help the needy by using local labor and materials. I was also taught to respect local customs. The last thing children in a Third World orphanage need is to feel that their language and beliefs are being wrested from them. They have already lost so much.

After graduating in 1992 I set my sights on Majune, an especially impoverished area in the low, hot northern region of Mozambique. The orphanage would essentially be a one-woman operation, so I needed to find support from some of the locals. That's why I was so thankful to God for sending me my assistant director, Crispo.

Crispo spoke five tribal languages in addition to English and Portuguese. Whether bargaining for a part for our pickup truck, procuring supplies for the orphanage, or negotiating the maze of Mozambique politics, he was the one I counted on day-to-day since we opened in 1995. Without his skills—and his deep love for the children who kept pouring through our gates—the orphanage would never have made it.

Early one July morning in 1997, Crispo had gone with Janito, a local farm worker, to tend some game traps set along the nearby Lugenda River.

That afternoon I was just beginning to wonder what was taking them so long when I heard Janito shouting breathlessly as he dropped his bicycle.

"Crispo snake bit!"

Seeing Janito's look of panic, I didn't need to ask what kind of snake. The black mamba is the most feared animal in sub-Saharan Africa. Growing as long as thirteen feet, it can travel as fast as a man can run, and delivers one of the world's most lethal bites. Even if the venom itself isn't fatal, a fast-moving infection can prove hazardous.

"We were checking the traps along the river when we surprised the snake," Janito explained. "A big one! It bit Crispo before we could get away."

During my first days in Africa, I'd had a wonderful donkey I christened Old Faithful. One morning I'd awakened to find the poor animal dead. Two ugly marks on his belly suggested the culprit was a mamba. The snake's venom is so powerful that human victims lose the ability to speak within minutes. Suffocation follows as the chest muscles stop working. Crispo could be dead already.

God, I know you always help me, I prayed. *Please help Crispo.* I grabbed the keys to the pickup and Janito and I raced to the river's edge.

Crispo was sitting upright on a log, staring into space with a glazed expression frozen on his face. Two bright purple marks were clearly visible on the back of his hand. His entire arm was swollen to twice its normal size, and was as hard as a tree trunk.

"Crispo, can you hear me?"

Nothing.

I'm a nurse. I didn't need to have the facts explained to me. I'd faced just about every problem imaginable in Mozambique: floods, infections, diseases, rebel attacks. Crispo had always been there for me. When others judged something impossible, Crispo said, "We will see, Miss Brenda." Now the man who had single-handedly done so much to make my dream of making the orphanage a reality could soon be gone. There wasn't a thing I could do about it. Nothing.

An idea occurred to me—an idea so outrageous, it could only have come from God. I had to say it out loud just to keep believing it: "Crispo! You are not going to die. Can you hear me? *You are going to live!*"

Mamba antivenin is costly to produce. I knew there wasn't a chance of us being able to find any. But we could at least get Crispo to a clinic. The nearest sizable one was in Lichinga, four hours away on primitive, treacherous roads. On the way we'd pass the village of Malanga, which had a much smaller clinic. Maybe we could pick up some antibiotics there to keep the infection at bay.

I put Crispo right next to me in the pickup, trying my hardest to keep him awake with a steady stream of talk as we lurched down the road.

"Crispo," I said, almost shouting, "I depend on you, and the children do too. You will live. You will not die." And with this thought came renewed faith. As Paul wrote, "In everything give thanks, for this is the will of God."

Lord, thank you for sending Crispo to help me. Thank you for his friendship over these years. Thank you for keeping him alive by the river long enough for me to reach him. Yes, I could be thankful even in this.

Crispo gave no indication that he understood my words. His breathing was labored, but he was still alive. "Breathe, Crispo, breathe!" I finally shouted at him. "You're going to make it."

I jammed on the brakes the second we reached Malanga, pulling up in front of the clinic in a cloud of dust. Crispo stirred. Amazingly, he turned and spoke clearly: "Miss Brenda, I feel better."

I was completely numb with shock. At the very least, Crispo should have been comatose by that time.

Some of the villagers had begun to gather around the truck sensing something was wrong. I couldn't believe my eyes as Crispo opened the passenger door and walked slowly up the stairs of the little clinic. That in itself was a miracle.

I raced inside ahead of Crispo. "My friend was bitten by a black mamba over half an hour ago," I hastily explained to the male nurse on duty. "He needs an antibiotic shot right now."

The man shook his head. "Every drop of our medicine is precious. We can't waste it on a dead man."

Crispo is not going to die! I reminded myself. "No!" I barked like a drill sergeant. "This man is going to live. We're not leaving until you give him that antibiotic." I stared determinedly at the nurse until he relented.

Crispo received his shot, and after refilling our water jug we got back in the truck for Lichinga.

Evening was coming on—always a dangerous time to be on the road in Mozambique. Not long after we left Malanga the sun began to set. We came to a long, rickety log bridge spanning a river. Normally we would have made a careful inspection on foot before taking the truck out onto it. Today there was no time for that. Foot by foot, I edged the pickup onto the bridge's crooked, hand-cut slats. The wood groaned beneath our wheels as we crept above the fast-moving water. Finally, the pickup's tires touched solid ground on the far side.

As we bounced along the rutted road, Crispo's lips and fingers began to turn blue. His skin felt dangerously cool, and his breathing became increasingly irregular. An hour passed and then another. Every few minutes I reached over and checked to make sure Crispo was still breathing. *Still alive, still alive.*

In the final hour of the drive, Crispo started to rally more and more. By the time we arrived at the hospital in Lichiga he was fully alert and awake. It was almost 8:00 PM—more than four hours since he had been bitten.

The town's generator wasn't working, and the hospital's small emergency room was lit only by a few solar lights. A doctor appeared and quickly examined Crispo's hand. The swelling had all but disappeared in the few hours since we had passed through Malanga.

"I assume this bite just occurred," the doctor said, writing in his chart.

"No, it happened at about three this afternoon," I explained.

"Impossible. If that were so, the arm would be much more swollen . . . and this man would probably be dead."

With God, nothing is impossible.

"I know it's hard to believe. But I'm a nurse, and I assure you he was bitten over four hours ago."

"Keep him still," the doctor instructed, shaking his head as he left the room. A little while later the doctor returned with another shot of antibiotics.

We spent the night at a nearby mission, and managed to make it back to the orphanage by early afternoon the next day. There, we found Crispo's relatives preparing for his funeral. When he stepped out of the truck, I thought all of them were going to faint.

The following morning I went to check on Crispo and found his bed empty.

"He already left for Malanga," Janito told me with a smile. "He said he wanted to see the looks on everyone's faces when they saw a ghost drive up on a motorbike!"

For weeks Crispo was a celebrity. "All I can remember from when I was on the truck was Miss Brenda telling me that I would live," Crispo said. Everybody wanted to see his wounds: the proof of what he had lived through. Our orphans were especially impressed. It was miraculous.

But what is still most amazing to me was that after Crispo was bitten I hadn't needed proof that he would survive. That was God's gift to me at the moment of my greatest fear. The facts had argued for Crispo's death, and faith had argued against the facts. For those four hours I clung to my faith, and against the odds Crispo lived.

I have always believed that without Crispo there would be no orphanage called Village of Love. Now I know that God believes it too.

One Phone Call

Susan Peabody

My teenage son Karl became withdrawn after his father died. As a single parent, I tried to do my best to talk to him, but the more I tried, the more he pulled away. When his report card arrived during his junior year, it said that he had been absent from classes ninety-five times and had six failing grades for the year. At this rate he would never graduate! I sent him to the school therapist, I grounded him, I even begged him. Nothing worked.

I hadn't prayed in years, but one night I felt so powerless that I got down on my knees and pleaded for help. "Please God, I can't do anything more for my son. I'm at the end of my rope. I'm giving the whole thing up to you."

I was at work when I got a phone call. A man introduced himself as the school guidance counselor. "I want to talk to you about Karl's absences." Before he could say another word, I choked up and all my frustration and sadness over Karl came pouring out into the ears of this stranger. "I love my son but I just don't know what to do. I've tried everything to get Karl to go back to school and nothing has worked. It's out of my hands." There was silence on the other end of the line. The guidance counselor solemnly said, "Thank you for your time," and hung up.

Karl's next report card showed a marked improvement in his grades. Eventually, he even made the honor roll. In his senior year, I attended a parent-teacher conference with Karl. I listened to his teachers marvel at the way he had turned himself around. On our way home, he said, "Mom, remember that call from the guidance counselor last year?" I nodded. "That was me. I thought I'd play a joke but when I heard what you said, it really hit me how much I was hurting you. That's when I knew I had to make you proud."

Karl had become a good student at school, and that was when I became a real student of prayer.

DIRECTORY ASSISTANCE

Beth Ann Batt

We live on an island in Lake Erie, and during tourist season work is booming. But winter is a lean time for my husband and me. One November several years ago I worried about how we were going to make our car-insurance payment.

I am not one to pray for things. So it surprised me when I got the idea that all I had to do was ask God for help. I sat down at the kitchen table and cleared my mind. Then I let my thoughts flow freely. *Lord, please send me work,* I prayed. *I will put my heart into anything that's given me. And if you can, make it something I can do with my children tagging along.* I focused all of my being on my request for a little while. Then, feeling peaceful, I let it go.

Not even half an hour later the phone rang. "Do you know anyone interested in delivering phone books on our island?" a woman asked.

"Me!" I almost yelled. She gave me more details. A few days later I met with the district manager, and he hired me on the spot. Curious, I asked how his company had come to call me for the job.

"Call you?" he said. "We only advertised this position in the mainland paper."

That afternoon I set out, four-year-old Jacob and nine-month-old John in tow. Together we delivered six hundred phone books door-to-door.

Within two weeks my paycheck arrived—exactly enough to cover our car insurance. I wasn't surprised. I knew someone had my number.

Doggie Do

Bonny Sparks

Last November my granddaughter Candy called me, asking about a prayer her three-year-old son, Chandler, was learning at school. "The prayer ends with 'Thank you, God, for everything,'" Candy told me, "but I can't remember the words to the rest of it, and Chandler doesn't remember either. Do you know it?"

I racked my brain. "That sure sounds familiar," I said. "Let me think on it, and I'll let you know if I can come up with something."

The next morning I took my nine-year-old sheltie, Ginger, to the grooming salon to get her monthly bath. Then my husband and I ran over to our church to help set up some items for the annual yard sale.

I'm usually good at remembering things. But try as I might, I couldn't come up with those words. It was driving me crazy. *God,* I finally prayed, *you're going to have to tell me the words to that prayer for Candy, because I sure can't remember what they are.*

Later that afternoon I picked Ginger up from the doggie salon to take her home, and noticed that the groomer, as usual, had tied a little scarf around Ginger's neck, this time a beige one. Ginger jumped into the car, barked happily and wagged her tail, smelling sweetly of shampoo and conditioner.

That evening when it was time for Ginger to go to bed I untied the scarf and folded it, wondering what I'd do with it. Put it in a rag drawer? Use it for tug-of-war with Ginger?

There seemed to be some words printed on it. I unfolded it and read: "Thank you for the world so sweet, thank you for the food we eat, thank you for the birds that sing, thank you, God, for everything."

Because it was so late I decided to e-mail my granddaughter. "You'll never guess what I just found," I wrote.

BOTTOM OF THE NINTH

Bruce Rice

I love baseball cards and I love collecting them. I've loved them all my life, just like my dad. But that autumn day twelve years ago was different. I'd come to work early at my sports cards-and-collectibles shop. Owning the store had been a dream come true. But I'd purchased thousands of baseball cards in anticipation of a big summer sale and, just as they arrived, major-league baseball went on strike. The World Series was canceled. Kids turned away from the game. My sales dove.

I stared at the walls, countertops, display cases—all of them filled with my beloved vintage cards. *Lord,* I wondered, *why did I go into this business? Wasn't this what I thought you were blessing?*

I'd been a successful shoe-store manager for twenty years. I put in long hours, but I was happy to continue at it the rest of my career. I'd never thought of a job in sports memorabilia. To me baseball was a passion, something to share with my children. At night I'd pull out a box of cards, sit on the floor with my three kids and tell them stories about favorite players and old nemeses, the way

other dads shared bedtime stories. "That's Bill Maze-
roski, second baseman for the Pittsburgh Pirates," I'd say.
"In 1960 he hit the home run that beat the Yankees in the
World Series." I'd grin and then add, "The rat."

Our life in San Antonio was wonderful. My wife,
Debbie, and I loved our community and our church. I
made a good living in the shoe business. Now and then
I'd visit a collectibles shop and buy a Cal Ripken, Ozzie
Smith or Roger Clemens card for the kids—players I
thought might one day win election to the Hall of Fame.
I was content, blessed.

In 1993 the roof fell in. Management at work
changed. I was laid off. Debbie was worried. "We need
your income," she said.

I'd seldom been out of a job before. But I saw this
as an opportunity. I started looking for a shoe store I
could purchase. Then, one day, a business associate approached. "Hey, I know you're looking to buy a business,"
he said. "Well, there's a San Antonio sports-card shop for
sale."

I raced home. "What do you think, Debbie? This is
the best chance we'll ever have to buy our own business," I
said. "Something the whole family can share in. It'll give
me more time with the kids."

We thought and prayed about it for a week, and then
agreed. "I know this is your dream," Debbie said.

We bought the place and spruced it up. Slowly, but surely, collectors came in—and not just baseball fans. I carried stuff from every major sport.

I spent most of our revenue on new inventory—the sports cards and autographed memorabilia. I anticipated that 1994 would be a big year for baseball, and I wanted to be ready, so I invested heavily in the baseball side of things.

That spring, we started out like gangbusters. Players were slugging home runs left and right. San Diego Padres outfielder Tony Gwynn seemed on target to become the first player to bat .400 for a season since Ted Williams did it, in 1941. "Debbie," I said, "I'm going to sink every penny we can into buying inventory. We have to strike while the iron's hot."

The card shipments arrived in August. The pennant race was heating up, the home-run hitters kept slugging, Gwynn's batting average hovered around .400. "We're going to have a great two months," I told Debbie. "This will push us over the top."

If only I'd known. Days later the baseball players went on strike and, for the first time ever, the baseball commissioner canceled the World Series. Sales stopped cold. We went from selling three hundred dollars' worth of baseball cards a day to five dollars' worth. We burned through our business account, and then through our personal account.

After one particularly bad Saturday, Debbie totaled up our meager sales for the day and began to cry. "Honey, we're going to go bankrupt," she said. "We're going to lose everything."

I put on a strong face, but inside I was as frightened as she. *We're down to one hundred dollars in our checking account. What happens if the roof leaks or the car needs a major repair? How will we pay for it?*

The next morning our refrigerator broke. The repairman said it would cost two hundred dollars to fix. So on that baseball-less autumn day I went to the store early. I needed to think. I looked around at my beloved cards, thousands of them, and collapsed into a chair by the counter. *Lord,* I begged, *I can't pay for the refrigerator. I can't provide for my family. I don't know if I should sell the store or try to see this through. Please show me a sign. Something. Anything.*

The phone rang. It was a stranger on the line. "Do you have Troy Aikman's rookie card?" she asked. Aikman was the Dallas Cowboys' star quarterback. His rookie card was worth a pretty penny.

"Sure do," I said.

"How about Emmitt Smith's rookie card?" Smith, too, was then a Cowboys star.

"Yes, ma'am, I have it," I responded.

She told me she would be right over.

Half an hour later a well-dressed woman and her teenage son breezed through the door. "Let me see those Aikman and Smith rookie cards, please," she said. Then the two of them started opening boxes of football cards, going through them like kids at a carnival. They whooped and laughed, pointing out this player and that. I mean, they carried on quite a bit. It seemed almost unreal.

The woman handed me a credit card. "Bill me five hundred dollars and tell me when we've used it up," she said. She and her son turned their attention back to the cards. Looking at the fun they were having, at the bond they shared, reminded me of myself and my dad— of myself and my own kids. I remembered why I'd purchased the business in the first place: to have more time with my family. *Lord, thanks for reminding me.*

The woman bought seven hundred dollars' worth of cards! After she left, I figured out my profit: $201, one dollar more than the bill for the refrigerator. That dollar meant as much to me as a million. It was a sign. I called Debbie. "Pay the bill. We have the money. We're going to be okay."

Twelve years have passed. We're still in business and we're doing well. Debbie and I raised our kids as much in the store as we did at home. It was like our second living room.

One day my kids asked me about the strange lady. She's become a bit of a legend in our family, like one of those old baseball heroes on my vintage cards. I told them the story again. "I think about her every day," I said. "I only wish I could thank her. She came into our lives when we needed her most, and I've never heard from or seen her again."

· 7 ·

KEEPING WATCH

"ARE NOT FIVE SPARROWS SOLD FOR TWO COPPER
COINS? AND NOT ONE OF THEM IS FORGOTTEN
BEFORE GOD. BUT THE VERY HAIRS OF YOUR HEAD
ARE ALL NUMBERED. DO NOT FEAR THEREFORE; YOU
ARE OF MORE VALUE THAN MANY SPARROWS."

—*Luke 12:6–7*

Lord, you know our comings and goings;
you know our fears and distresses.
Thank you for your watchful care.

ROUND-THE-CLOCK CARE

Susan Oliver

My daughter, Anita, and I are nurses. So when Anita's twenty-one-year-old son, Justin, sustained massive head and brain-stem injuries after a horseback riding accident, we knew there was little chance he'd survive, much less wake from the coma. For ten days the family kept vigil at the hospital. Then Anita and Doug, Justin's dad, made the painful decision to take Justin off the ventilator.

Miraculously, Justin started breathing on his own. "Still, he could stay in the coma indefinitely," the doctor said.

"I want to bring him home," Anita said. I put my arm around her. I'd help, of course. We couldn't change Justin's condition, but we could take care of him and love him round-the-clock.

Anita and I prepared her house for Justin. Doug and the paramedics wheeled him in a few days later. "We had quite a surprise this morning," Doug said. Justin's eyes were open! He had come out of the coma. Doug told us what had happened. "The prettiest woman came into his room and touched Justin's face. 'This young man's been assigned to me,' she said. 'I will follow where he goes.' She said no more and left. Not a minute later Justin opened his eyes."

Today Justin is twenty-three years old and runs marathons. I like to think his angel runs too, following wherever Justin goes.

"STOP, THIEF!"

Linda Lawrence-Winters

Limited tickets for the White House tour were handed out early, so my friend Susan and I got going before 7:00 AM. We hadn't come all the way from Texas to miss our chance to get in.

It was a chilly morning, and everyone on Pennsylvania Avenue was bundled up. "Hold your purse close," Susan murmured. "I've got my whole life in my bag, and those kids are watching us." She nodded toward a couple of menacing-looking teenagers.

We crossed the street. Just as we got to the curb, Susan stumbled and fell. "Stop, thief!" she yelled. The kids had pushed her down and were running away up the hill with her purse.

"Stop, thief!" I yelled, tearing after the kids. *Lord, help! I'll never catch them!*

People on the street took up the call. "Stop, thief!" they yelled, pointing at the purse snatchers. The kids weaved in and out of the crowd, knocking everyone aside. They disappeared over the top of the hill. As I staggered up, out of breath, a man appeared in front of me. He was dressed crisply, all in white with not even a coat—strange on a day like this. He handed me Susan's purse!

Susan limped up behind me. "Can you believe it?" I said, handing it to her. "This man here . . ."

I gestured beside me. The man in white was nowhere to be seen.

MY TREE-STUMP ORDEAL

Bryan Wolfe

Seven years have passed since that fateful July day, but I still shudder when I think about it. It should have been a delightful Saturday morning excursion with my two-year-old daughter, Brittany. Her mother, Tracy, was sound asleep, having just finished her night shift. So I decided to take Brittany out for a drive in our Datsun pickup. I had about six hours until I needed to show up for my shift at the plywood mill where I operated a forklift. Figuring we would be back before Tracy awoke, I didn't leave a note.

As we drove down the highway Brittany laughed and pointed. "Da-da, see moo-cows?" Her love for animals reminded me of a beaver pond I knew deep in the woods; I thought she would enjoy seeing it.

We peeled off onto a gravel road and after a few miles turned down a dirt lane. I shifted into four-wheel drive and picked our way through towering firs until we reached a clearing. The beaver pond sparkled in the sun.

It was about 10:30 AM, and I figured we could stay an hour before making the fourteen-mile drive home.

We didn't see any beavers, but Brittany loved splashing her hand in the water and calling to them. I could see the pond was quite deep. I led her back to the truck, and after settling her in her car seat, I stood for a moment savoring the beauty around me. The dense Oregon forest was so peaceful. Birds called from giant trees; patches of sun glowed on the pine-needle carpet. As I drank in the fresh air, I caught myself thinking of the God who had created all this.

I quickly shrugged the thought away. God and I hadn't been on speaking terms for a long time. I couldn't see myself obeying him in everything. Besides, I figured, if I was ever to get anything out of this life it was up to me. I had done all right too: I had a good woman, a sweet daughter and a decent job. And here I was doing what I liked best, enjoying the outdoors.

Then I thought of my new rifle hanging in the cab of the pickup. With Brittany safe in her car seat this would be my chance to try it out. I picked up an old quart-size plastic bottle that was lying nearby and filled it with pond water. I also found an empty beer can. Some sixty yards from the truck loomed an old gray-red Douglas fir stump that had been left by loggers. It stood more than six feet high and must have been at least fifteen feet around. An earthen bank behind it offered a perfect safety buffer. I set the bottle and can on the hollow stump's rim, went back to the truck and, resting my rifle on its hood, picked both off with one shot. It felt good; the rifle was zeroed in just right.

My targets had toppled down inside the trunk. Curious to see where I had hit them, I set the rifle on the hood, and then went and angled over the stump's rim. Balancing on my stomach, I leaned way down when...

Crack! The rotted wood crumbled under me and I plummeted headfirst into the hollow stump. I was three quarters of the way down, and my right arm was wedged between the wood and my body. But I could use my left. I started pushing when *whump,* I slipped all the way down. My head smack against the bottom, my right arm still trapped.

Now I'm really in trouble, I thought. It was a Saturday; I knew no one, including loggers, would be around. Gritting my teeth, I tried to push myself up and then hook my toes over the stump's rim to hoist my body, but it was hopeless. I was wedged like a cork in a bottle. I slumped for a moment, panting heavily. The pungent odor of rotted wood filled my nostrils, blood pounded in my head and sweat burned my eyes. Panic began to flood me as I fought claustrophobia. I struggled to free myself again when I heard a sound that froze me.

"Da-da? Da-da?" It was Brittany! She had got out of her car seat and was toddling around looking for me. She could fall into the beaver pond. Like a trapped tiger, I struggled in blind fury, but the jagged wood biting into my body only wedged me in tighter.

"Brittany!" I cried. "Stay by the truck!" Could she hear me? My voice was muffled inside the thick-walled stump.

In terror I continued struggling. As rotted wood crumbled under my flailing left hand, I thought, *That's it! I'll dig myself out.* Clawing viciously at the moldy porous wood, I sought to open a hole large enough to wriggle out. But cruel reality struck when my nails hit the trunk's hard outer wood.

Panting, I collapsed. Wood dust half blinded me. Parched, I grabbed the water-filled bottle, which had only been grazed by my bullet. But my bloodied fingers couldn't open it. Almost three hours had gone by. I slumped hopelessly, only to flinch from a new sensation: bugs! Insects were crawling all over me.

I shuddered, nauseous from the humid heat, stench, and being upside down. Bile burned my throat and I vomited. While coughing, spitting and brushing ants from my sweating face, I realized I had not heard Brittany for a long time. What had happened to her?

"Oh, God," I cried, "please take care of my little girl. She is so innocent. Take me instead, a sinner, but save her." I broke down sobbing. "Please forgive me for turning my back on you." Then, succumbing to my plight, I lost all control, screaming from deep within my soul until my throat was raw and I could only gasp for God to forgive my sins.

It was then the words "The Lord is my shepherd" came to me, from having recited the Twenty-third Psalm as a child. Over and over I found myself mumbling, "The Lord is my shepherd...the Lord is..." and I sank into oblivion.

I was roused by the sound of a man's voice. "Hey, buddy, you want some help?"

Was I hallucinating? But I heard the voice again. Someone was there!

"Yes, please...help...me," I groaned.

Strong arms grabbed my boots and lifted me from the stump. Reeling, I couldn't stand. My swollen head felt like a pumpkin. Two men comforted me and called 911 for an ambulance. I looked around wildly. "Brittany!" I rasped. "Brittany!"

One of the men carried her over to me. She was peacefully asleep. I was so grateful. It was 5:45 PM. I had been stuck in that stump for more than six hours.

"What? How?" I gasped, turning to my rescuers. They introduced themselves as forestry workers, Thomas Soward and Terry Knight. They had parked a bulldozer a distance away and for some reason felt led to walk down to the clearing.

"We saw your truck," said Thomas, "but didn't pay it much attention. We were about to leave when we spotted the rifle lying across the hood. That got us to looking around, and there was your little girl asleep in a mossy ditch. When we saw your shoes we figured at first someone had left them resting on the stump and gone swimming.

"The Lord sure was watching over you both," he added.

Not until later did I realize how much of a shepherd the Lord had been. He had led Brittany to a safe place, and kept me alive until the two men found us.

It took being stuck upside down in that tree stump—helpless—to get me to admit I couldn't get everything out of life on my own. Now I thank God for it all: my wife, my daughter—and my life.

The Longest Steps

Elizabeth Guarino

It was time to admit I needed help, but I wondered if anyone could really understand what I was going through. My husband, Dan, had driven me to the 12-Step meeting, yet I couldn't bring myself to go inside alone. We sat in our car, and I rolled down my window to get some air. Dan tried to encourage me, but someone who didn't share my problem could only understand so much. I was on my own.

"Hello," came a cheery voice. A young woman leaned into my window. "My name's Sunny," she said. "Going to the meeting?"

"I'm afraid my wife's having second thoughts," Dan said.

"You can change if you really want to," Sunny said. "Come and meet some people who already have." Her openness was hard to resist. *At least I won't be walking in there alone,* I thought. I got out of the car and followed her to the meeting.

Sunny seemed to know everyone there, and with her by my side I felt at ease.

"You'll be back for next week's meeting, right?" Sunny asked me on the way out.

"I sure will," I replied. Sunny waved good-bye. Dan was waiting in the car. "I'm proud of you, Elizabeth," he said. "And grateful that Sunny showed up when she did."

I stuck with the 12-Step meetings, but never saw Sunny again. My friends in the group claim not to know her. They deny ever having seen her. In fact, they insist I was alone at that first meeting. The meeting that changed my life.

FEAR AT THE WHEEL

Marsha Gubser

Vacations usually presented an unexpected challenge or two, but I was always up for an adventure. I'd grown up in the wooded mountains of California, where bears and bobcats were a fact of life. We often got six feet of snow in the winter. One time I got frostbite on my toe trudging through the snow to increase our water flow, which came from an open ditch several miles away. In good weather, jumping my horse over fallen logs with my girlfriend was a regular after-school activity.

Our family—my husband, John, and our four kids, ranging from ages six to eighteen—lived in a much more comfortable environment, but I liked us all to enjoy a healthy dose of nature now and then. God had made a beautiful world and I wanted to see as much of it as we could.

We'd braved thunderstorms en route to Oklahoma and bat-infested caves in Oregon together. Now we were headed out to the desert to a breathtaking spot—Utah's Bryce Canyon. My parents had taken me to this national park nine thousand feet above sea level as a little girl. I could still remember the mazes of canyons and the enormous "hoodoos," odd-shaped spires that rose out of the limestone and towered over us.

We got an early start and ate breakfast on the road. John was at the wheel. Within a few hours, the combination of fast food and driving had taken its toll on him. "Honey, would you take over?" John asked. "I think I could use a nap."

"Happy to." We pulled over at a rest stop to switch drivers and made it a bathroom break, figuring once we got into the park there wouldn't be as many facilities. Once everyone was settled back in the car, we seemed to make it to Bryce Canyon in no time. I loved a good steady stint behind the wheel, and was still raring to go.

The road was narrow, winding up the vertical canyon wall, which rose several hundred feet. The valley floor dropped far below on the other side. It was easy to see all the way down to the bottom. Not even a guardrail blocked the view.

"Awesome," the kids kept saying in the backseat. I glanced at John, fast asleep in the passenger seat. The canyon was just like I remembered it. Redder than you could capture in a photograph. Hot, so hot that you could see the heat waves, making everything look surreal. What

I hadn't remembered was how steep this road was. It almost didn't seem possible that we were safe driving on it. We seemed to be defying gravity in our big, heavy automobile. I gripped the wheel tighter and leaned slightly toward the windshield. *You're a competent driver,* I told myself. *Try to relax.*

But I couldn't. No matter how hard I tried. *Lord, be with us on this road.* I kept my prayers to myself. I didn't want to scare the kids. Over and over I asked the Lord to keep us safe. But somehow I couldn't feel his presence.

My eyes kept straying over the edge of the road. How could there be no guardrail? One false move and we'd go over. My confidence was draining fast.

I came to the first switchback, an inside curve. The road climbed so sharply that making the turn I saw the pavement rise straight up in front of me. The road was chopped off by the clear blue sky. It appeared to end in midair. It looked as though I would drive off into space. I knew that wasn't true, but I *felt* it was. I clutched the wheel. I let up on the gas pedal. We lost speed.

"Mom, what's wrong?" my oldest asked. My youngest began to cry.

John woke up and seemed to read my mind. "Quiet down," John said. "Your mother needs to concentrate." He put his hand on my shoulder. "You're doing fine, Marsha. Just follow the road."

I managed to nod my head. There was no room to pull over. I had to keep going. I kept my eyes fixed on the road in front of me—directly ahead, not farther on, where it looked like a drop-off into nothingness. I made the next curve. And the next. No one said a word. Finally, I saw a turnout. "Let's take a breather," John said. I pulled over, relieved.

We got out and walked around a little. John put his arm around me. I was disappointed in myself. And in my unanswered prayer. I was still shaking. John drove the rest of the way.

That night in the motel, I couldn't sleep. Every time I closed my eyes, I saw the edge of the road curving into space above the canyon. And every time I felt the same panic I'd felt when I was driving. I'd let fear overcome me.

Where were you, Lord, when I was so afraid? I closed my eyes again.

The exact same image of pavement and sky filled my mind once more. But this time there was a guardrail. Not an ordinary guardrail. Tall angels lined the rim of the road, forming a protective barrier between safety and a plunge into the deep valley below. My fear vanished with the fading vision.

That was the last time I let fear rob me of my self-confidence and my faith that God was always with me, ever near, watching over me and keeping me safe. With my fear, I had built a wall that had separated me from his constant love and protection. The next day our family returned to Bryce Canyon, and it was even more spectacular, now that I imagined it filled with the Lord's angels, watching over us in the beautiful world he made for us to enjoy.

Fear Takes Flight

Vincent Yeo

I'm a motivational speaker, flying all over the country giving speeches. But for years I had a terrible fear of flying. My hands would sweat and my pulse would race the minute I reached the jetway. *This is irrational,* I'd tell myself, but it made no difference. The fear was overwhelming. I'd grip the armrests till my knuckles turned white. Takeoffs and landings were particularly hard. The irony of giving speeches to help other people yet having such a crippling fear myself wasn't lost on me.

I began to pray every Sunday, asking God to remove the fear. But months passed and my fear remained. Then one Sunday, kneeling beside my wife in church, I looked up. At that moment, a man stood several rows in front of me. He turned and smiled at me, and then walked up the aisle, stopped at my pew and handed me what appeared to be a business card. Then he continued up the aisle. *How odd,* I thought. I finished my prayer, stood and glanced at the card. "Dear God," it read, "please protect me while I travel to do the work you've given me and bring me back home safely to my family." I turned to look for the man, but he was gone. "Maybe he was an angel," my wife said. I wasn't sure. But I tucked the card into my wallet.

On my next flight I pulled out the card and read it while waiting for takeoff. Though my pulse raced, I could feel my nerves calm. On the following flight, I felt less anxious. Finally, one day, without being aware of it, my fear left. No more gripping the armrests or sweaty palms.

The card is dog-eared and worn now, but it's still in my wallet. I don't know what ever happened to the man who gave it to me. But I know that that Sunday he was an answer to my prayer.

"CALL AL"

Rebecca Yauger

The doorbell rang just as I was about to go to bed. *Strange.* I peered out the window. What was an elderly woman doing on my porch at that time of night? She seemed upset. Her hair and clothes were disheveled. I opened the door.

"Can I help you?" I asked. The woman stepped right into the foyer as if she knew where she was going. Then she stopped and looked around, a confused expression on her face. "Where's Al?" she said. "I want you to call Al."

"Who's Al?" I asked her. She stared at me and didn't answer, so I repeated the question.

"My son-in-law," the woman said. "Al's my son-in-law. I want you to call him." Her voice wavered. She sounded like she was on the verge of panic.

I tried to get her to sit down, but she only became more agitated. I brought her a glass of water. That didn't help either. She just repeated the same thing over and over again. "Call Al. I want you to call Al."

"What's Al's last name?" I asked. She looked at me blankly. Suddenly she said, "Sanders. Al Sanders."

"Al Sanders? I know that name!" I said. "I work with an Al Sanders." I ran to my desk where I kept the company directory. I pulled it out, looked up Al's number and dialed.

"It's Becky from work," I said when he picked up. "I know this sounds crazy, but there's a woman at my house who says that she's your mother-in-law and . . ."

"Thank God!" Al exclaimed. "You're an answer to prayer, Becky. I'll be right over. Please tell her I'm on my way."

Al's mother-in-law was as happy to see him as he was to see her. Al explained that she had Alzheimer's and had wandered away from her nursing home. This wasn't the first time, either.

"She's never gone this far, though," he said. "The nursing home is almost three miles away from here. She had to cross the main boulevard. But it's a miracle that out of all these houses she came to yours. Who else would have had my number? It's unlisted."

"Walk with Me"

Mike Osuch

In the first light of dawn I stood at the Reflecting Pool at the outer edge of the Vietnam Veterans Memorial in Washington, DC. I had driven all the way from California to see it, but I couldn't bring myself to take the final steps to the wall.

I had fought in Vietnam as an eighteen-year-old and it was there that I had started using drugs. One night I convinced my friend Gil to take my patrol duty while I went off to get high. Gil was killed that night. Back home, after the war, I hopped from town to town and jail to jail, tormented by guilt and unable to beat the addiction that had caused so much pain in my life.

Now, twenty-three years later, I had come to find Gil's name and confront the wreckage of my past. This could be my last chance to start life over. But I couldn't approach the wall.

Through the morning haze a man walked toward me. He looked like an ordinary government worker in a suit and tie. "Walk with me," he said, and without a thought I did. Together we walked along the path. Then we stopped and the man held his hand over some names on the wall. "You'll find him here," he said.

I looked up to where his hand had been, and there among the fifty-eight thousand names cut into the black granite was Gil's. Staring at the spot, I knew that nothing I could do would ever erase my friend's name from that wall. The only thing that could change was me. With God's help, I could start today.

As the sun broke over the Potomac, I turned to my guide, but he was gone. Today I would like to tell him how my life has changed. But first I would ask him how he knew where to look for that one name.

Deer Crossing

Patrice Vacca

Moving from urban New Jersey to the Pennsylvania woods was a dream come true for me. The land around my house was a campground in the summer. My nearest neighbor was miles away, and there was no phone service to my house. Didn't bother me a bit.

Back in New Jersey I'd worked as a rehab nurse. I saw people all the time. Some predicted I would soon tire of my new solitary life, but I hadn't so far and didn't expect I ever would. All my life I've felt connected to nature, and I could never feel lonely with animals nearby. The woods were full of them.

"I call that one Scarbelly," I told a visiting friend when a deer tiptoed out of the woods one afternoon. She was a doe, easily recognizable by the old wound running from her shoulder to her hip. "She had a fawn last year. She brings her baby around too."

"They sure seem to like you a lot!" she said as the doe inched nearer to me. We stayed very still so as not to startle her.

"I'd like to think so," I said. "Deer aren't easy to get close to."

Each day I woke up in my house in the woods was a pleasure—until one April morning. I heard the birds singing as usual, saw the pale sun through the window, smelled the fresh air. But something was wrong. I tried to sit up. My legs felt like lead. They refused to cooperate with me. I had to struggle just to swing them over the side of the bed.

I managed to stand. *Get to the bathroom,* I thought. Just turning in the right direction almost knocked me over I was so off-balance. I managed to shuffle toward the bathroom door.

Thud.

My shoulder hit the doorjamb. *How could I miss the door?* I took a step back and tried another time. Once again my shoulder hit the door.

I didn't feel it at all. In fact, I couldn't feel my shoulder, my arm, my fingers on the left side of my body. It was like a great emptiness hung where my arm should be. I tried to squeeze my fingers together. They wouldn't budge.

Stroke! I thought, my nurse training kicking in. My mother and grandmother had both died from strokes. Could that be happening to me—at forty-six? I had to get to a hospital fast. But how? No neighbors, no phone . . .

"Well, God," I mumbled, "we've got to do something here. I need help!"

I pulled on the easiest clothes I could find and slipped my feet into sandals. I moved carefully to the door.

"Scarbelly!"

The old doe was waiting on the deck. Her fawn stood at her side. Four more deer crowded behind them.

They weren't the rescue team I'd imagined, but they were all I had. "Look, I have to get to a doctor," I said. "Now."

The deer flicked their ears, watching.

If I could just get to the road at the top of the hill, I thought, *I could flag someone down.* Could I make it that far? I had to try. The longer I went untreated the worse the damage could be. I moved stiffly off the deck and onto the lawn, forcing my left side to move. The deer were close behind me.

The lawn stretched out before me like an ocean. *I'll never make it all that way!*

I put my hand to my face, ready to cry. *That won't help!* I told myself. I rubbed my eyes and looked down at the gravel road. I was standing at the edge of it. I looked over my shoulder at the expanse of lawn and my house in the distance. *How in the world did I get here?* I didn't remember walking that significant distance—and it would have taken ages. But here I was, and so were the deer—right beside me. Scarbelly's deep brown eyes looked into mine. "Did you carry me?" I asked.

She blinked her long lashes. She was so close I could have touched her.

A cloud of dust in the distance! I waved frantically as the car got closer. The driver smiled and waved back at me, but he didn't even slow down. *He couldn't even tell I need help!*

Another car went by. The same thing happened. Again and again.

"I have to go out to the middle of the road," I said. "They'll either stop or run me over. If I don't get help I might not make it anyway."

I pulled myself into the road. The herd of deer walked forward, keeping pace with my own tortured steps. They huddled close around me, surrounding me with a protective circle in the middle of the road. The heat from their bodies warmed me. Their soft sides rose and fell in a calming rhythm. I felt their gentle breath on my skin.

A truck appeared in the distance, moving toward us. *If this one doesn't stop I don't know what I'll do.*

I raised my hand and held it straight out in front of me. The deer stood still as stone, not budging even as the truck came at full speed. Thank goodness, it slowed and stopped. The driver stuck his head out of the window and stared at me, a woman surrounded by a herd of deer.

"Please," I said, "I need to get to the hospital. I think I had a stroke."

The driver's eyes moved to the deer and back to me. He opened his mouth, but no words came out. He shook his head and climbed out of the truck, hurrying to open the passenger door.

The deer parted to let me get to the truck. The driver eyed them the whole time he helped me inside. The deer eyed him too, but they didn't run away as they usually did when faced with people. People besides me, that is. The driver got me safe in the passenger seat and got behind the wheel. He shifted into gear and beeped the horn as gently as he could. Only then did the deer lower their heads and step gracefully off the road.

I lay my head against the car seat, exhausted. *Thank you, God*, I prayed, *for your beautiful creatures who watched over me like you do.*

Tests at the hospital proved I had had a stroke. "You should have a good recovery," the doctor told me. "You're lucky you were able to get here as quickly as you did. If you'd waited you might have had serious long-term damage."

I might have been lucky, but the situation was nothing short of angelic.

"*I* Can Handle It"

Dave Kenshol

I used to travel a lot when I was a regional manager for Sears. Once I had a last-minute meeting at our corporate headquarters in Chicago. While weaving my way through the bustling Sky Harbor Airport in Phoenix, I thought of all the things that could mess up the trip—delayed departure, bad weather, broken equipment. That got me thinking about the flight my grandmother Maude Staunifer would soon be taking. Grandma had been living with my uncle Ray for several years here in Arizona, but now, at ninety-eight, her health was failing. We'd decided to move her into a nursing home that was close to three of her sons and their children and grandchildren, instead of being near just Ray and me in Arizona.

Knowing how happy Grandma would be surrounded by family, I was certain it was the best thing to do. The only thing worrying me was Grandma's flight to Chicago. Both Ray and I worked long hours at our jobs, and Grandma, never wanting to inconvenience anyone, refused to allow either of us to take time off to accompany her. "I can handle it," she had assured us.

Reluctantly we agreed. But now that I was at the airport myself, I was having second thoughts. Had we made a mistake in giving in? So much could go wrong, and I wasn't sure Grandma would be able to manage alone, despite her protestations to the contrary. *God, maybe you can find someone to help look after her,* I prayed.

Since I'd left the final details to Ray, I didn't even know when Grandma's flight was. *I'll call Ray after I land,* I told myself, trying to push my worries out of my mind as I made my way to the gate. At the check-in counter two people were in line ahead of me. I overheard the man trying to arrange seating for an older woman in a wheelchair. She was going to be on my flight to Chicago.

I reached out and took the handles of the wheelchair from the man, telling him, "Ray, why doesn't Grandma sit next to me?"

· 8 ·

Fulfilling Dreams

"The Lord bless you and keep you;
The Lord make His face shine upon you,
And be gracious to you."

—*Numbers 6:24–25*

*Lord, I thank you for your blessings—in your mighty
and mysterious ways, you fulfill our dreams and
desires, sometimes large, sometimes small.*

Feeling Close

Ann-Marie Walker

Twice a year Gary and I took the kids and made the twelve hundred-mile trip up from Alabama to my native New England to visit my folks, crowding into their cozy little house on Cape Cod. I loved those trips. One year my daughter, Michelle, gave me a ceramic cottage that looked like one of the saltboxes on the Cape, with cedar trees on either side and a quaint old rowboat out front. "So you can feel close even when you're in Alabama," she said. I gave Michelle a big kiss and a hug in return.

We all got older. I worried about Mom's worsening diabetes. Dad had a heart attack. Suddenly, they were facing a move to the nursing home.

"I can't let that happen," I told Gary. "Let's move up north and take care of your parents," he said. Our kids were grown by then. It was possible.

We put our things in storage and moved into my parents' basement on Cape Cod, but it wasn't quite the same. The vacation cottage was way too small for the four of us to live in full-time.

Gary and I had to find a place of our own. The houses we saw were too expensive or too far from my parents. I tried to take comfort in my favorite Scripture, from Jeremiah: "For I know the plans I have for you, plans for well-being and not for trouble, to give you a future and a hope." But the longer we looked, the more I wondered what lay ahead for us. For my parents.

One summer day the Realtor showed us a saltbox house down the road from Mom and Dad's. It was lovely. Even better, I had a tremendously warm feeling about it, like those old vacations. I couldn't explain it.

What a relief to finally unpack our things! They'd been in storage so long it was like seeing them for the very first time. Except when I unwrapped the ceramic cottage my daughter gave me. I turned it over in my hands. The sloping roof, the shutters...it was an exact replica of our new house, right down to the cedars and the quaint rowboat the previous owners had left on the lawn. A future and a hope. It had been there all along.

$\mathcal{P}$URRRRRFECT

Althea Kaye

$\mathcal{I}$ lived on my own, and for months I'd been feeling lonely, so much so that I prayed about it. Finally I decided to get a cat. But I put off going to the pound. It wasn't just any cat I wanted. I was holding out for a friendly all-black tom with six toes. (I had heard six-toed cats have the gentlest dispositions.) I already had a name picked out: Aiisi.

One afternoon I was in my study working at my computer. I was on a tight deadline with a project. I distinctly heard a male voice say, "Go get a cat." Almost by reflex, I replied, "Okay, as soon as I finish this." The voice repeated, "Go get a cat." It was clear he meant *now*.

No more than forty-five minutes later I was at the pound. A young woman showed me the cats. I shook my head. None of them was Aiisi. Finally the woman asked, "Do you have something specific in mind?"

"This might sound odd, but..." I told her everything on my list.

She gave me a strange look. "Follow me," she said. She led me to a cage in back. A black ball of fur was curled in the corner, purring like a well-tuned sports car. The woman opened the door and lifted him out. "Yup, he's a male," she said. I noticed his extra-large paws. Six toes!

"He's the one."

"He was brought in just forty-five minutes ago," the woman said. "Perfect timing."

And how!

MESSAGE IN A BOTTLE

Eredis Gutiérrez Aguilera

When I look back on how I came here from Cuba, I can't help but feel my steps were guided. Each piece of the journey has clicked into place as if part of a design, a larger plan. Still, some might be tempted to call this blind luck. Not I.

My homeland of Cuba is a beautiful island. By far the best thing about my country is its people. It took all of my will to decide to leave the land and the people I love, especially my family. Many times it seemed easier to simply remain in Cuba and hope that someday things would change, that the people would be given freedom to believe and say what they wish.

I grew up barely aware of who or what God was. God seemed as far away as the America I sometimes dreamed about, as remote as freedom itself. Then my friend Rebecca revealed something to me that changed my life...the first step of my journey.

My goal was to study medicine but I would have to pass a very tough university entrance exam. In the library with Rebecca one day, I was overwhelmed with anxiety. I confided in her how afraid I was that I'd fail. She looked at me for a long time as if trying to make up her mind about something, and then leaned over and whispered, "Eredis, if you do not know the answer to a question on the test, ask God to help you." Then she quickly turned back to her book.

Not many people in my country talked about God. I didn't know what to think of what she'd said, but I kept turning it over in my mind. Then, while taking the grueling test, I came to a math problem that completely baffled me. I couldn't even understand the question, let alone come up with an answer. The more I thought, the more panicked and confused I became. *If you miss this question, you will never go to medical school,* I warned myself. As I racked my brain for an answer, Rebecca's words came back to me. *Ask God to help you.* I had never talked to God before. Now, desperate, I said a clumsy prayer for help, almost as if asking for a big favor. "God, whoever you are, I want to be a doctor. It is my dream. Please help."

Rereading the question, I knew at once what was being asked. I wasn't sure of the answer, but I understood the question and that was a start. When the test results were posted, I had passed—by just the margin of answering that one question.

I wanted to find out more about God. Rebecca gave me a pocket New Testament. Then I found an old Bible in a bookstore and began to study it. I learned that prayer is so much more than merely asking a favor of God, and that sometimes prayers are answered in ways that are mysterious to us. But God knows our desires at all times.

From then on my dreams no longer seemed so far-fetched. There was a lottery to choose some of the twenty thousand Cubans who would be permitted to immigrate to the US that year. Along with thousands of Cubans, I applied and dreamed of being chosen. Now I could do more than dream. I could pray!

At Mariana Grajales University in Holguín City, I studied medicine—and prayed—every day. I had little time for anything else. And while I was getting closer to becoming a doctor, I was getting no closer at all to America. One weekend in February 1997, my third year of studies, I decided I needed a break. I went to my grandmother's house near Playa Larga.

At dawn that Saturday, I stood on a patch of beach, fishing the churning surf. In the distance two freighters inched along, the smoke from their stacks smudging the rosy sky. Behind them, the rising sun rippled on the horizon. Somewhere beyond that was America. Lately I had begun to think that I was not meant to go to America, that God did not share my dream. *Lord, what is your will?* I asked now, looking out at where the water met the sky. *Where do I belong?*

A burst of sea spray forced my gaze down at the sand. There, among the debris cast up by the Atlantic Ocean, was a bottle. Not an unusual sight on a beach. I was about to kick it back into the water when I noticed a piece of paper inside, with writing on it.

I dropped my fishing rod, picked up the bottle and sat down on a rock to examine it. A crack in the seal had allowed some water in, but the cork was intact. Holding the bottle up to the dawn sky, I tried to read what was written on the paper. From the little English I knew, I could make out the words *note* and *open*. My heart raced. This bottle probably came from America!

I broke the bottle on the rock as gently as I could and took out the paper. I couldn't wait to get back to the university, where I had my English-Spanish dictionary, so I could decipher the note's message.

After my patient rounds on Monday, I began to translate the note from the bottle. A family by the name of Lieske from Henderson, Minnesota, had put the bottle in the ocean near a place called Cape Cod, Massachusetts, on July 30, 1993, during a family vacation. The Lieskes asked that the person who found the bottle write to them, stating where the bottle had washed up and telling a little bit about himself. They promised to write back.

I went to the library and checked an atlas. Henderson was almost as many miles from Cape Cod as Cape Cod was from Cuba. This bottle had come so far! It must be very cold in Minnesota, I decided, looking over the map. *They probably get snow there.* I'd always wanted to see snow. I traced the 1,600-mile route from Cape Cod to Cuba. The bottle had taken three years, six months and fifteen days to reach Playa Larga. Just the thought of such a journey brought butterflies to my stomach.

This bottle traveled all the way from America, I kept thinking, *to land at my feet on a beach in Cuba.* That night in my prayers I asked, *Lord, is this a message?* Did it mean I was destined to go to America, that God shared my dream?

I wrote the Lieskes and we exchanged photographs. They said I should visit them if I ever came to America, and that they were praying for me. Just knowing about those prayers made my dream feel more within reach.

A year after finding the Lieskes' bottle I was walking home from school when a neighbor stopped me. "Eredis," she cried, "you've been chosen!" She was so excited that I could hardly understand her. Then another neighbor rushed up and explained that my name had been drawn in the immigration lottery.

I had read about miracles in my Bible. This, I realized, was what a miracle felt like. I ran home. My mother was crying. I took her in my arms. She was torn between wanting what was best for me and not wanting me to leave. Someday, I told her, Cuban mothers would no longer have to face this choice.

I had to wait several months for my paperwork to be approved. I began to feel sad that I would be leaving all my friends and family. As long as the Castro government was in power, it would be nearly impossible for me to return to Cuba. Yes, I had wanted to go to America, but I didn't realize that it would feel so lonely. Though I did not want to seem ungrateful, I told God of all my fears and asked if he could help me. I believe this is why I met Naillyvis.

Again, it started with a neighbor's announcement. The daughter of her cousin had also been chosen in the immigration lottery. That was certainly enough to catch my interest. When I heard that this young woman was also a medical student at Mariana Grajales University, I couldn't help but think of the Lieskes' bottle. Was God again leading the right people into my life at the right time?

"What's her name?" I asked.

"I can't remember," my neighbor said, but she'd try to find out. I went to my classes thinking about how good it would be to have another student to travel and plan with, if only I could find her. Then came the day of my formal interview with the immigration officials. Sitting in the waiting room was someone I recognized from class, a woman I'd known and liked for quite a while.

"Naillyvis!"

"Eredis!"

Naillyvis had been very quiet around the university about her good fortune, because it is not in her nature to brag. Now we could go to America together.

There is something about planning a journey that brings people closer. Naillyvis would probably say it is the romance of travel. It wasn't long before we fell in love, and the stress of leaving Cuba was replaced by the sense that we were being guided to where we were meant to be.

The day of our departure, I rode in the back of my uncle's open truck with half a dozen relatives. At the airport I climbed down and gave a little speech thanking my family for all their love and support. I tried not to cry but it was no use. Taking my little sister Liset aside, I gave her my Bible. "Liset, read this book and trust in God. He has a dream for you too."

Naillyvis and I held hands and closed our eyes as the plane rumbled, then roared down the runway. I thought about Rebecca teaching me to ask God for help, about the Lieskes in Minnesota and how their bottle gave me a message of hope when I needed hope the most, about finding Naillyvis—about all the wonderful things that had happened. When I opened my eyes again, Cuba was falling away below, a shrinking patch of green in a blue sea. America lay ahead. Once more I thought, *This is what a miracle feels like.*

Editor's note: Eredis and Naillyvis made it to America safely and later got engaged. While they study English and apply to medical school here, Eredis works in a glass factory in Louisville, Kentucky, and Naillyvis is a hotel maid. In December 1998, the Lieskes flew Eredis and Naillyvis to Henderson, Minnesota, to spend the holidays with them. And it's there that Eredis finally saw snow.

CASE CLOSED

Paulie Panek

$\mathcal{I}$ was going through a rough patch in my life and thought a weekend getaway to one of Minnesota's lakes might lift my spirits. I signed up for a retreat set up by my church. On the way we skirted the town of Brainerd, and a lonely stretch of road where my mom died in a terrible car accident when I was seventeen. Recalling that horrible day made me feel sad and more down than ever. The question that had haunted me for more than twenty years came back: Did Mom die all alone? I'd thought I could find comfort in the answer, but since no one was able to tell me what had happened, that answer never came. My prayers seemed in vain.

At the retreat center I was assigned a room with several other women. One of them, Terri, had come all the way to the retreat from Midland, Texas. "What brings you to Minnesota?" I asked her.

"My mother lived near Brainerd," she told me.

"Really? I used to live near there."

"Mom passed away four months ago," Terri said. "After the retreat I'm going to visit her grave."

I remembered how hard my first visit to my mother's grave had been. Even after all these years the grief felt fresh. My mom was still such a presence in my life that it almost felt as if I could never completely stop mourning her. I knew what Terri must be going through. Before we got ready for bed that night, I decided to tell her my story.

"A man lost control of his car, crossed the centerline and hit my mom's car head-on," I said. "That's what I was told. I wasn't with her when it happened."

"When was that?" Terri asked.

"November of 1973."

Terri looked shocked. Then she took my hand. "Paulie, I was the first person to stop at the scene after the accident. I was young, but I remember your mother well. I held her hand and prayed until the paramedics took her away. I was there."

Mom had not been alone. At last I had the answer, and the comfort I was searching for.

TWICE BLESSED

Lucille Lind Arnell

$\mathcal{P}$eople could have mistaken my sister, Mae, and me for twins, except that Mae was a year older, taller than I was, and quite thin. We did everything together. We had the same friends, went to the same college, and even met two great guys at the same time and got engaged. There was just one problem: money. Our parents couldn't afford two weddings back-to-back, and our fiancés were still in college. "Why don't we have a double wedding?" I suggested. "It would help cut costs." Mae was all for it.

When it came to planning, we tried to be as thrifty as possible. But the one thing we couldn't double up on, obviously, was the gowns. We wanted two reasonably priced dresses that would look similar. Since our builds were so different, I knew it wasn't going to be easy. We looked in bridal shops and department stores, but nothing on the racks appealed to us. And there was no way we could afford custom-made dresses.

"Please help us find the right gowns," we prayed with our fiancés one night.

The next day at school, I had a soda with my classmate Jean. I started telling her about our wedding plans. "My sister and I had a double wedding too," she told me. "We'd be glad to let you use our gowns." The only thing was, Jean didn't want the dresses altered. *They'll never fit,* I despaired, but Mae and I had nothing to lose by trying them.

A few days later Jean handed us two beautiful dresses. Mae slipped hers on and gasped, "It's perfect!" Then I looked at myself in the mirror and couldn't believe it. "They're *both* just right," I said. When we walked down the aisle that June day in 1957, our dresses looked like they were meant for us. I believe they were.

HAPPY BIRTHDAY, LEWIS

Abbie Daigle

I am spending a year working and living at the St. Francis Inn, a soup kitchen and an outreach to the homeless on the east side of Philadelphia. It's in the Kensington neighborhood, an area so rough that the police nicknamed it "The Badlands"—abandoned houses, prostitution, drugs, poverty. The landscape is bleak and depressing. Which is just why I had to move here. I wanted to help people caught up in such circumstances.

One of my duties as a volunteer at the Inn was to drive a van from supermarket to supermarket, collecting much of their donated food. We got all kinds of things, from canned goods to day-old rolls. And we put everything to good use.

But one day last fall I picked up something that made me feel so sad. It was a beautiful birthday cake, with blue and yellow frosting on top. "Happy Birthday, Lewis," read the bright script on top. *Poor kid never got his birthday cake,* I thought. I put the cake in the van, said a quick prayer for Lewis (whoever he was, wherever he was) and finished up my rounds.

Back at the Inn, I stacked the birthday cake up with the other food we would be distributing.

Later that afternoon I was back at the Inn, sorting mail in the office, when Sister Janette walked in, wearing a triumphant smile and carrying the cake in her arms. "Look what came in today!" she exclaimed. "It's a birthday cake! Can you believe it?"

Sister Janette worked with the neighborhood children. She reminded me about the mother who had called her the other day, asking if there were any way she could get something for her little boy to take to school to help celebrate his birthday. Like most families who came to St. Francis Inn, they had nothing.

"Perfect," I said. Or almost. Well maybe we could scrape off the name that was on the cake.

Sister Janette opened the lid of the box to take a look. "Oh my!" she said, gasping. "My little Lewis is going to be so happy!"

The Wedding Spot

Samantha Irwin

$\mathcal{I}$ opened the letter from my brother Scott and immediately wondered why he had sent it. Nestled in the envelope was a tiny classified ad, no bigger than a quarter, offering an old hotel for sale: "Balch Hotel, built 1907, national register of historic places, twenty-one rooms, Dufur, Oregon." "Thought you might be interested," his note read. Huh? True, my husband, Jeff, and I had thought about buying property to open an outdoor wedding venue—for a few years we had been praying about whether I should quit my job as a middle school teacher to try another line of work. But an old hotel? What would we want with an old hotel?

Actually, the letter hit me more deeply than that. Truth was, I had begun to wonder whether even dreaming about a new life was foolish. I was thirty-six and had taught for thirteen years. A few years previously, I had gone part-time, sensing that I needed more balance in my career. I knew what I was good at—organizing projects, preferably outdoors, working with my hands. But with teaching, I had begun to feel increasingly frustrated. Just when I got comfortable with a curriculum, I was switched to another grade level, subject or class, the fate of part-timers. Jeff and I had been asking God to show me my gifts and how to use them. I was waiting for a door to open.

I'd thought I'd found that door when my sister got married. I helped plan the wedding and discovered I loved planning, coordinating and hosting. The day of the ceremony, we drove to a secluded spot above the Columbia River Gorge, a lake ringed by wildflowers and evergreens. I stepped out of the car overwhelmed by beauty, and the feeling only intensified as I watched guests similarly awed, and fussed over my sister in an elegant, tile-lined outdoor changing room. *I love this,* I thought. *I wonder what it would take to run a place like this.* As my two brothers rowed my sister across the lake toward her fiancé, I felt a dream take shape. Planning weddings combined everything I enjoyed—being outdoors and gathering countless strands together into one special, beautiful day for other people. What could be better?

I helped organize my friend Deborah's wedding a year later, and that sealed it. Jeff and I began praying seriously for the right door to open, a piece of property we could buy and turn into a wedding venue like the one my sister used. We didn't have a lot of money so we needed to plan carefully before I quit work. I took a community college class on running a business and even asked an architect to draw up provisional designs. We found some lovely locations for sale, bid on them and—nothing happened. "I don't understand why you're not getting counteroffers," our real-estate agent told us. We found other spots, only to discover zoning restrictions blocking our way. What was going on? I had felt so certain. But doors were closing, not opening. Then Scott's letter arrived.

I showed the letter to Jeff. "I think I know this place," I said. I had been to Dufur, a button-cute farm town surrounded by rolling wheat fields, a few times on trips as a child. Our family owned property nearby. We'd stop for breakfast at a restaurant across the street from the Balch Hotel. I remembered peering inside with my father, awed by the lobby's marvelous, solid-wood front desk.

"Well, it can't hurt to have a look," Jeff said. "It's only forty miles away. It'll be a fun day trip. Maybe the grounds are what we're looking for."

I wondered. Running a hotel was not the dream we had talked about. Ushering couples into a sun-drenched meadow was. Still, we both loved the area, and I figured we should at least check it out. We made an appointment.

We set out on a bright May morning, meandering past shimmering wheat fields until Dufur appeared, a little more than fourteen blocks wide, no bigger than in my childhood. We drove up Main Street, and there it was, a beautiful, three-story brick building with the words "Balch Hotel" painted in old-fashioned letters just below the roof.

We got out, and a real-estate auctioneer ushered us through a back door into a cavernous dining room. It was beautiful, but empty. "The owners ran this place for twenty years," the auctioneer said, "and did a lot of restoration work. But they've had some health issues and decided to sell. So far, we've only managed to auction off the furniture. They're waiting for a cash offer." Our feet echoed on luminous fir floorboards as we passed into the lobby. Instinctively, I looked for the front desk. It wasn't there. Lacy curtains glowed in sunny front windows. Across the street, I could just make out the restaurant we'd gone to for breakfast.

We mounted the stairs and peered into bare rooms. I pictured a bride doing her hair, looking out at the grounds below where a wedding party gathered. Jeff and I had always loved historic homes. The Balch, I realized, was like an amalgam of everything that made old architecture wonderful. Lath and plaster walls and ceilings. Wobbly century-old glass. Sculpted window frames made of fine-grain wood, so much lovelier than today's fast-growing, mass-produced lumber. Surfaces were worn with a patina from banging luggage, swinging latches and dings from shoes. Everything, it seemed, told a story, decades of stories. The previous owners had begun the laborious process of stripping the layers of paint from wood surfaces, revealing gorgeous hundred-year-old fir. I began daydreaming about continuing the job. *Wait, what are you thinking, Samantha?* I looked at Jeff again. He was grinning. I felt myself smile too. The auctioneer, I realized, had moved on to another room. Jeff drew close. "What do you think?" he murmured. "This place is amazing."

I drew a breath. "I think so too." By the time we reached home in Hood River, our heads were swimming with possibilities.

We began canvassing banks for a loan. Everyone turned us down, skeptical we could make money hosting weddings in an old hotel that hadn't been open in years. Desperate, we drove back to the Balch to meet with Howard Green, the owner, to ask him what to do. The minute we arrived, my carefully rehearsed speech flew straight out of my mouth. Howard, it turned out, reminded me of my father, a man raised in the Depression, canny, a bit ornery, but with a love for old things, a sharp eye for authenticity and a low tolerance for baloney. He greeted us warmly and took us through almost every room, telling stories and pointing to where his wife, Patricia, had hung the hotel's laundry to dry on a clothesline outside. They adored the hotel, he said, and had put it up for sale only after they'd had some health problems.

Then he got to the point. "You've been very transparent with me," he said. "I'll be the same with you." He showed us some documents, gave us some financial advice and, in the end, he and Patricia dropped their demand for cash and helped us find financing. Three months after that first trip to Dufur, I met Howard in the Balch's gravel parking lot. He enveloped me in a bear hug and handed me the keys with a loud, "Am I looking at the new owner of the Balch Hotel?" I felt positively giddy.

I left my teaching job, and we put our Hood River house up for rent and moved into a bare room at the Balch. While Jeff commuted to his job, I threw myself into restoration: scraping, stripping, sanding, varnishing and sanding some more. I painted, learned plaster repair and, with help, picked out and arranged antique furniture. The night before our first wedding, Jeff and I were still out helping the landscaper pack the last of his tools by the glare of his truck's headlights. Nevertheless, the ceremony went off without a blemish. The bride dressed in the third-floor suite and the couple said their vows under the shade of fir trees.

That evening I went over some paperwork behind the front desk in the lobby, the big front desk, the one from my childhood. Howard, it turned out, had saved it from the auction, just in case whoever bought the building decided to keep it as a hotel. I stand behind it every day now (we run the Balch as a wedding venue and as a bed and breakfast), seeing not just its smooth, worn wood, but the lesson it stands for. God *does* open doors—just not always the ones we envision. Mine came in a cryptic little envelope from my brother Scott, a clipping about an old hotel that needed new owners, and a chance to change our lives.

Just a Trifle

Heather Lynn Ivester

Maybe next year," I said to my husband, Andrew, one night as I punched numbers into a calculator. Andrew and I had always dreamed of going away someplace special for our tenth anniversary, but with four kids, my mother's illness and a pile of bills, our dream seemed impossible. *Please, God*, I prayed, *we need a break. But I can't figure out how to make it happen. Can you help?*

A few days later I took my daughters grocery shopping. "Mom, please, can we buy this tub of meringue cookies?" one of my girls pleaded.

"I don't think so," I said. No room in the budget for trifles. Just then, the funniest feeling came over me. I looked at the bright pink and yellow cookies and saw my girls' bright smiles... and I tossed the cookies into the cart. When we opened the lid at home, I noticed a small advertisement for a recipe contest.

"Look, girls," I said. "They have a cooking contest for recipes with these cookies." What to make? A cake? Ice cream and meringue? "Let's have a party." Then I remembered my grandma's trifle. I created a dish using the

cookies, and set up a tea party complete with pink flowers and balloons. My girls giggled as I took their picture
while they enjoyed my "Miss Meringue's Magical Vanilla
Rainbow Trifle." *Not a winner,* I thought, *but at least they
should see what fun we've had.* I sent the photo and a copy
of the trifle recipe to the contest.

I was so surprised when I answered the phone one
day to hear a voice say, "Congratulations. You're the grand
prizewinner of our contest." I'd won an all-expense-paid
trip for two to Santa Barbara, California. I gave him my
anniversary date. "That's perfect," he said.

A prayer, a tub of cookies, a recipe for trifle and a need
to get away. Somehow they all connected into a dream
vacation that was a godsend. Literally.

THE SOUND OF LOVE

Leslie Ackerman

It had been love at first sight when Bill and I met almost sixteen years ago. I graduated from high school six months early so I could marry him as soon as possible.

We wanted to start our family soon after our wedding, but found out we could never have children. So we threw ourselves into our careers. He farmed the Illinois land that had been in his family for generations, and I worked my way up to head of marketing at a company in our hometown. The job became my top priority, and our marriage started to fall apart. Eventually we separated and then divorced.

With my marriage over, I jumped at a career opportunity that would take me to Atlanta. But the job didn't turn out as I had expected. Far away from my family, friends and the man I had loved, I sank into a dangerous depression.

Bill kept trying to convince me we could get back together. One night he called while I was sitting on the floor by my bed. I picked a fight. We argued until finally Bill shouted, "What do you want from me?"

"If you really loved me you'd be here!" I screamed. I hurled the phone across the room. I fell on my face and cried, "Lord, I'm miserable!"

Instantly the phone rang. It was Bill. "I'm on my way," he said. That was all I needed to know. (Months later Bill and I remarried.) But as I reached to put the phone on the nightstand, I froze: When the phone rang, it had been off the hook.

· 9 ·

KEEPING SAFE

For He shall give His angels charge over you,
To keep you in all your ways.

—*Psalm 91:11*

*Lord, we may be unaware of the many times you've
protected us from harm in the past—thank you.
In your mercy, protect us again today, preventing
missteps, warning of dangers, keeping us safe.*

WHO'S CALLING?

Keith Pulles

It's time to shock the pool and shut it down for winter," Dad said that September day. He was right. You could feel the nip of fall in the air. But to me, at age nine, closing the pool meant summer was definitely over. I wasn't sure what "shocking" meant. "All it means is using special strong chemicals to clean up the water," Dad explained. "That way the pool will stay in good shape even though it's covered all winter long."

Dad went out to the yard and I watched glumly from the window as he opened a jug and started dumping stuff into the pool. Then he got another jug. More stuff. *That's a lot of stuff to put into the pool,* I thought. Just then the phone rang. I ran to check the caller ID. "Unknown name, unknown number," flashed back at me. Normally I only picked up the phone when I saw it was someone I knew. Mom and Dad had warned me about talking to strangers. But that day a voice inside said, *Pick it up!* The urge was so strong and insistent, I lifted the receiver to my ear. "Hello?"

"May I speak with Steve Pulles, please?" I didn't recognize the voice. A telemarketer, probably. They were always calling. Dad wouldn't want whatever it was this guy was trying to sell. But again, something made me open my mouth and say, "Hang on. I'll go get him."

I went outside, through the garage door, phone in hand. "Dad! Phone!"

"Who's calling?" he hollered to me.

"Dunno."

Dad walked around the side of the garage from the backyard and took the cordless from me. "Hello? Hello…?" A couple of seconds later he took the phone from his ear and turned it off. "Nobody there," he said.

Suddenly there was an enormous boom from out back. "The pool!" Dad shouted. Turned out he'd mixed together two chemicals he shouldn't have. The mixture exploded out of the water, leaving toxic fumes. The fumes dissipated, but… "If I'd been out here," Dad said later, "I could have died."

Unknown caller? I don't think so. The person on the phone that day certainly had our number.

Water!

Diana Eckles

After dinner I read the paper until I began to nod off, and then climbed the stairs to bed. I set my alarm to go off early to give myself a few extra precious minutes in bed in the morning. I have a hard time waking up and I'm well acquainted with the snooze button. That night, I fell quickly into a deep, dreamless sleep.

When I woke, though, it wasn't to the buzz of my alarm, but to an extraordinary thirst. I felt as if my throat were burning. All I could think about was getting to the jug of ice water in my refrigerator.

I never get out of bed during the night, not even to go to the bathroom, much less to get a drink. I rolled over and tried to ignore the urge. *I need to get my sleep,* I thought. *Otherwise I'll be a mess tomorrow.* But by then I was wide awake, and fixated on getting a glass of cold water.

Finally, I gave in to my craving. I threw off the covers, got up and headed downstairs. Then I saw it: a glow from the kitchen. *A flame!* I had left a candle burning on the table, right on top of a cotton mat that was about to catch fire. I rushed to move the candle, but the glass holder was so hot I couldn't pick it up. I grabbed pot holders, whisked the candle to the counter and put it out.

While staring at the wisps of smoke rising from the extinguished flame, I marveled at my close call. It wasn't until I was on my way upstairs to get back into bed that I realized I hadn't gotten the glass of water I'd been dying for. But I no longer needed it: The overpowering thirst that had driven me out of bed had evaporated.

GIDEON'S SWORD

Mavis Gustafson Pigford

"I'm not supposed to give these away," the young man said, handing me a display Bible, "but I sense you should have this." I shrugged and absently tucked it away. We had a Bible at home. I'd only stopped by the Gideons' table because nothing else at the Iowa State Fair was set up.

A few days later I was walking to town when a car pulled up beside me. "Get in," the driver snarled, pointing a gun at me.

I did as he said. Soon he pulled over, grabbed me and tried to force me down on the seat. I struggled with all my strength. Finally he ordered me out of the car.

Before both my feet were on the ground, I heard a shot and felt a sharp pain in my side. I collapsed, and the man came around the car. He picked up my purse, took out my wallet, and then threw the purse on my head and shot it. I felt a dreadful impact. Still conscious, I lay silent, hoping he would think I was dead. I heard the car drive away, and I stumbled to a nearby farmhouse. A woman called for help, and the police and an ambulance arrived shortly. Even as I was being rushed to the hospital, the police were closing in on the drug-crazed driver based on the description I'd given them.

At the hospital, just before I went into surgery to remove the bullet in my side, my sister came to see me. "Do you know what saved your life, Mavis?" she asked.

She handed me the Bible that had been in my purse. A bullet was lodged inside, its tip stopping exactly at Psalm 37:14–15: "The wicked draw the sword, and bend the bow . . . to slay those whose ways are upright. But their swords will pierce their own hearts, and their bows will be broken."

Saved!

Patricia Brandt

Oregon or bust! A neighbor let me borrow his Volkswagen microbus to motor up the California coast. Those old hippie-mobiles were the way to travel back in the 1970s. At twenty-one, I was a flower child, single, with a brand-new baby girl. Life was going to be one big adventure.

Growing up I'd taken things way too seriously. Especially my faith. I believed with all my heart. It was as natural to me as breathing. One day when my teenage problems threatened to overwhelm me, I asked God to hold me in his hands. It worked somehow. I'll never forget how clear and calm I felt. I almost thought I heard God say, "I will always be here with you."

But a lot was happening out in the real world. The Bay of Pigs. President Kennedy's assassination. The turmoil of the civil rights movement. Drugs. Vietnam. The protests. It seemed there was nowhere to turn for solace. Everything came to a head in 1966, when the cover of *Time* magazine asked, "Is God Dead?" The consensus seemed to be that either God was dead or he'd never existed in the first place. I was on my own now, and I wanted to know the freedom people my age were talking about. Freedom from the tired rules of the older generation, freedom from religion and self-deception and work that was meaningless. Life was supposed to be a great adventure, not a chore.

I left home and threw myself into the ways of the new generation. My daughter, Rain Ivana, was born in 1971. I named her Rain because I hoped she would help me grow. She was really all I had to depend on. And she depended on me.

Now Rain was four months old, about to go on her first big trip. I stuck a Baby On Board sign on the back of the VW, and wedged an old padded playpen between the front and back seats. Rain cooed at her toys and slept, and I drove four hours straight, to our first stop, Santa Barbara, a quaint seaside town with avocado groves stretching up to the hills. We got out at the historic Santa Barbara Mission. "We'll visit here for a while," I told Rain, "then set up camp on the beach."

I carried Rain through the beautiful rose garden and walked into the chapel. It was quiet, empty but for us. Candles burned, the hopes and prayers for loved ones. I moved into a narrow pew, Rain in my arms. On one wall was a painting of the Virgin Mary. The other showed a portrait of the Crucifixion. A cross hung on the wall behind the altar. *God, are you here?* I reached to pull down the kneeler in front of me—but then stopped myself. "God isn't here," I told myself. "He's a myth." Rain and I were just tourists. Like everyone else who came here to see art, architecture and history. But why did I remember so well how it felt to be held in his hands? Didn't I want Rain to know that kind of love? In all my free-spirit living I'd yet to experience anything so fulfilling.

"Let's go get set up for the night," I told Rain. "We have a lot to think about."

I'd seen cars parked right on the beach. Fresh salt air and the sound of the surf would be the perfect lullaby. I carried Rain back to the microbus, set her in her playpen and headed for the shore.

At the beach, kids played, parents barbecued, dogs chased Frisbees. I pulled the VW onto the sand and parked not too far from the water. This would be home for the night. All these fun-loving folks would be my neighbors. We'd watch the sun go down. Somebody was sure to start a campfire, and we'd gather around it to sing. Maybe this was all my baby and I needed.

Rain napped, and I read till the sun sank toward the horizon. A lot of people were packing up to go home. *Other commitments*, I thought. *Not me. I'm free to watch the stars come out.*

I climbed into the microbus to set up the sleeping bag and lantern, and then fed Rain. By the time we came out everything had changed. I looked left and right. Not a single person, not a single car. There was nobody on the beach!

"I guess sometimes free can mean lonely," I explained to Rain. We looked out at the waves. Was the tide coming in? I wondered if I should move the bus farther back, maybe even off the beach entirely. "What do you think, Rain? Should we go?" She looked at me so trustingly. Waves lapped closer and closer.

"Okay, let's go." With Rain safe in her playpen back in the VW, I got behind the wheel. Turned the key in the ignition. Nothing. I tried again and again. No use. The engine was dead. I got out and stood in front of the bus. Waves lapped at my heels. Push! I shoved as hard as I could. The thing wouldn't even budge.

The beach was desolate. Not a soul in sight. I'd never make it to the road in time to flag down help. Water was already up to the tires. *You have to stay calm*, I told myself. *For Rain.* I stared out at the ocean. So big and dark, and I was totally at its mercy. Free? I wasn't free. That was the myth. I was lost and alone and powerless.

"I was wrong, God," I called out to the water. "When I was a teenager you promised you'd always be with me. I turned away from you. And I'm so sorry. Please help us."

Calm washed over me. The same calm I remembered from so long ago. Then I noticed something strange in the water. Two rubber pipes extended above the surface, a couple of yards apart. They moved together, closer and closer to shore. Then two huge shapes rose up amid the waves. Divers!

I ran to them. "My car won't start. Could you give me a push?" I begged.

The men towered over me, both more than six feet tall, their wet suits glistening in the setting sun. They pulled off their masks. One had long blond hair and the other had beautiful brown hair. And their eyes! Both had the brightest eyes I'd ever seen, crystal-clear and shining like sapphires. Eyes full of light and strength.

Without a word the men walked up to the microbus, one on each side. I got inside with Rain and put the van in first gear. The engine sparked to life, and with a whoosh I was up on higher ground, safe from the rising sea. I waved a thank-you out the window. The two men walked away side by side, disappearing into the night.

"Well, we're back on our adventure," I told Rain. "But now we're going to get serious about how things really are." Someday, when she was older, I'd tell her all about this night. The night God sent his angels to prove he'd been looking after me—after us—all along. I was saved in more ways than one.

ON COURSE

Kathleen Boudreau

$\mathcal{M}$y family was camping at a lake in central California one summer when my teenage daughter, Cassie, cruised up to shore on our family Jet Ski. "Hop on, Mom!" she yelled over the engine noise. I hesitated. I'm a little scared around mechanical things, but Cassie was an ace. I climbed on and off we flew.

After half an hour of zigzagging, we stopped at a little island in the lake. Cassie secured the Jet Ski, and we sunbathed for a while. By the time we headed back, I was thoroughly enjoying the ride.

Then, on one turn, the Jet Ski tilted sharply. We lost our balance and toppled into the lake. The machine righted itself and, engine still roaring, raced away from us. We watched the Jet Ski streak across the lake. There was nothing to stop it!

God, please don't let it hit anyone, I prayed. *Guide it.* Cassie and I reluctantly started the long swim back to shore. But after just a few strokes I heard a sound. I shot a glance over my shoulder. "It's coming back!" I yelled. The Jet Ski was charging directly at us. I drew Cassie close to me, the two of us transfixed by the sleek, powerful machine bearing down on us. I had a terrifying vision of it slamming into both of us as we bobbed there in the water. "God, help us!" I cried out. Suddenly the Jet Ski slowed down and then stopped completely—just a few feet from us.

Cassie and I looked at each other. The Jet Ski couldn't possibly have run out of gas already. Maybe the key had fallen out of the ignition.

Cassie climbed aboard. "The key's still here," she said. Cassie turned the key and the engine sprang to life again. I hopped on behind her and we headed back to our camp.

Since that day on the lake I'm a little more confident and careful around mechanical things. And a lot more confident in the power of prayer.

STRANGER AT THE STATION

Julia Goodworth Sabol

There were no signs of life outside the station as I sprinted through the rain. I stepped off the bus with my suitcase over my head and made a run for it. Inside the heavy entrance door I found myself all alone in the huge terminal where I had to change buses. Deserted. That's how I felt no matter where I was these days.

I hadn't always felt that way. Since I was a little girl I'd been certain angels were watching over me every moment. Like the time someone whispered for me to wake up in the middle of the night and saved my whole family from a fire in our home. But where had that reassuring voice been when the doctor told me the child I was expecting would never come into this world? I took a trip to visit my family, hoping to find some peace. Now I was on my way back to my husband, but my heart was just as heavy as the day I left. God had always been there to guard against tragedy. Where was he now?

I looked around the waiting room, but saw only shadows, no people. It was one o'clock in the morning. Yet somewhere there was music playing. I followed the sound to a lunch counter at the other end of the terminal. A gruff-looking man was reading a newspaper. Apparently he was both the cook and the ticket agent.

"How long before the next bus to Petersburg?" I asked.

The man scowled up at the grease-covered clock on the wall. "Couple of hours," he mumbled, going back to his paper.

I returned to the dimly lit waiting area. There were rows of empty wooden benches. I found one near enough light to read, and pulled out my book. I'd only read a few lines when I sensed I was no longer alone.

Seven young men sat directly opposite me. Each one sat with his arms crossed, staring at me. I pulled my cardigan tightly around my shoulders, hoping another bus had arrived with more travelers. No, it was just me and this gang of men—and they weren't travelers. They were obviously here to start trouble, and there was no one to protect me from them.

Hands shaking, I closed my book and stood up. The gang stood up too. The lunch counter seemed miles away. I couldn't hear the music anymore. My heart beat so loudly I thought I would faint. I stepped away from my seat.

Footsteps behind me got louder—and closer. *Dear God, help me!*

A man appeared at the end of the row of benches. "There you are!" he exclaimed. I looked up into his smiling, handsome face. My heartbeat slowed. I'd never seen him before, but somehow he knew I needed help. "I've been waiting ages for you!" he said. "I was afraid you'd gotten lost."

The stranger was about forty years old with a strong, sturdy build—he looked like Superman! He picked up my suitcase with little effort and threw his free arm around my trembling shoulders. "Let's have a cup of coffee while we wait for your bus."

I didn't look back. By the time the stranger and I got to the lunch counter the gang was gone. The man behind the register perked up and brewed us a fresh pot of coffee. My companion didn't touch his cup, but we chatted until it was time for my next bus.

Dawn was arriving as he held open the station's heavy door for me. The storm was over, and my bus waited across the still-damp blacktop. As I got on board the stranger handed me my suitcase. I looked down to thank him, but he wasn't there.

As the bus pulled out, I thought about all the sadness I'd experienced over the last few weeks and thanked God for the angel who came to my rescue. God hadn't deserted me. He was watching over me still, just like when I was a girl. And that knowledge would see me through the many joys—and trials—of life.

He's All Right

Mary Jane Kelsch

My husband, Walt, and I live just down the street from the rectory, so when Father Nuwer caught pneumonia that March we offered to help in any way we could. We'd be happy to bring him a hot meal, take him to a doctor's appointment—whatever he needed. Walt and I were both retired, so we had plenty of free time.

"Don't hesitate to call on us day or night," Walt told Father Nuwer. "We are always here for you."

We were cleaning up after dinner one evening when the phone rang. It was Father Nuwer.

"I'm having trouble breathing," he said, his voice raspy and strained. "Can you drive me to the hospital?"

"I'll be right over," Walt said. He threw on his coat and shoes and dashed out the door.

Walt got into our car and headed for the rectory. I tried to watch some TV, but I couldn't concentrate on anything; I was too worried. Father Nuwer was asthmatic. I knew that if he had a serious asthma attack on top of his pneumonia, it could kill him.

I stared at the clock, trying to guess when they'd reach the emergency room and how long it would take to see a doctor. Minutes ticked by, then hours. It was nearly 11:00 PM. *Why hasn't Walt called?* I wondered. *Is Father Nuwer going to be okay?*

Just as I was about to shut off the TV, the phone rang. I grabbed the receiver.

"Walt?"

But it was my daughter, Donna.

"Don't worry, Mom," she told me. "The hospital just let me know that he's all right."

"Thank goodness," I said. "But why would the hospital call you about Father Nuwer?"

"Father Nuwer?" Donna asked. "He's fine. He must have had the hospital call me first. It's Dad. He had a heart attack. The doctor said that if they hadn't been able to use the defibrillator on him right away, he might not have made it."

Donna paused. "Lucky thing Dad was right there in the emergency room when it happened."

Lucky? I think it was more than that.

"NEXT THING I KNEW"

Margie Miyoshi

It was the afternoon of the annual sukiyaki dinner, my church's biggest fund-raiser of the year, where our predominantly Japanese-American congregation invites the community to share a meal. I was chair of the event and I had been busy all day getting food ready and organizing the other volunteers. Two of the people helping out had to leave, so I took them home. Driving back to the church along the four-lane highway, I was completely exhausted.

I felt my eyelids growing heavy. *Just a little bit farther,* I thought. *I'm almost there.* I turned up the radio and turned on the air. But the headlights blurred in front of me. Everything moved in slow motion.

The next thing I knew, there was a loud screeching sound, a heavy grinding from underneath the car, sparks flying. The car had run into the median separating the lanes of traffic. Instinctively, I gripped the steering wheel and steadied the car, my eyes open wide.

Thank God for that median, I thought, shaking. *I could have crossed into the other lanes and right into an oncoming car!*

When I got back to the church I told everyone what had happened.

"Was there a lot of damage?" Joe, a fellow volunteer, asked.

"I was afraid to look," I told him. We went back to the parking lot to check out my car.

What if it's serious? I thought. I braced myself for the worst. But to my surprise, there wasn't any damage to be seen. No scrapes on the frame, not a dent on the tire rim, not even a scratch. Joe and I looked underneath and around the car, but couldn't find anything wrong.

It's a miracle, I thought.

A few weeks later I was driving down the same stretch of road where I'd had my accident. *Maybe there's still some tire rubber on the median,* I thought. I kept glancing over along the middle of the road, curious to see where my car had hit.

I kept looking. But never saw it. There was no median to be found. Not even a sign of one.

THE DREAM

Jeanne Frois

For the hundredth time I glanced over my shoulder on my way to work. The business quarter was full of men in suits carrying briefcases, women in tailored skirts and sensible shoes. It was the same crowd I moved among Monday through Friday, but this particular morning I sensed danger lurking at every turn. The night before I'd had a horrible dream, and I couldn't seem to shrug it off.

It wasn't like me to be so fearful. I was in my twenties, doing administrative work in downtown New Orleans. The city had been experiencing a rise in violent crime, but I used my common sense and didn't take risks. The building where I worked was secure. At least that's what I told myself as I walked inside. A man held the door for me and flashed a smile. I looked at his eyes. No, those weren't the eyes from my dream.

Before I'd seen anything in the dream, I'd heard my father's voice: "Zsa-Ree!" He always shortened my French name, Jeanne Marie. No one had called me that since he died.

"Daddy?" I said in my dream. "Is that you?" But instead I came face-to-face with a pair of dark, menacing eyes. *Criminal eyes*, I thought to myself. *Cold and deadly.* I froze in fear.

"Watch out for these eyes, Zsa-Ree," Daddy warned. I wanted to run. But I stared at those eyes so I'd remember them like Daddy said. I jerked awake and couldn't sleep for the rest of the night. How would I make it through the day?

I stepped into the elevator and pressed 3. That was just like Daddy, telling me to use my head, to think before I acted. He used the same advice on the petty criminals and troubled youth he met on his beat. Daddy was a police detective in New Orleans—not an easy job. Daddy got knocked out in a Mardi Gras riot, shot point blank in the chest, and once caught a bank robber making a getaway. Daddy knew all about keeping people safe. Me, most of all. He tucked me into bed before going out on patrol. He always made the sign of the cross over me. "Dream about pretty things," he'd said before turning out the light. "God's angels will protect you while I'm gone." I lay back on my pillows. Of course I was protected. Daddy would never go out without leaving angels behind.

I missed Daddy terribly when he died, missed his jokes and his songs. I missed hunting for frogs and acorns together. But I still felt safe, as if Daddy had left his protection behind. Just like those nights when he made the cross over me before he went out on duty.

I walked off the elevator, still puzzling over why I'd heard Daddy's voice in such a frightening dream. "Use your head, Zsa-Ree," he'd said, just like when I was little. But use my head about what? Was I in danger? My heels clicked on the linoleum floor. I took a deep breath and opened our office door. I waved good-morning on the way to my desk. "It was just a dream," I muttered as I dropped my purse in a drawer. "Concentrate on your work."

That wasn't easy. The feeling of unease hung over me. At my desk, at the coffee station, even down the long hallway the led to the ladies' room. It was almost noon and I'd got almost nothing done. My eyes were puffy from not sleeping the night before. "I need to splash some cold water on my face," I told the woman at the next desk.

I wove my way around my coworkers and walked down the hallway. The sounds of typing, telephones and conversation faded behind me as I approached the ladies' room door.

I pushed it open. I was alone. I splashed some water on my face and held my fingers over my tired eyes. The door opened behind me, and I let my hands fall from my face. In the mirror was a man. He came up behind me—right behind me. So close I could feel warm breath on my neck. I turned around. The man towered over me. Tall as a basketball player and wide as a fullback. I looked up into his face, praying there was some reasonable explanation for this intrusion. Holy God, what does this man want with me?

I know those eyes. Cold, dark and criminal, just like in my dream. This was the danger I was warned about. Daddy's words came back to me. *"Use your head, Zsa-Ree."*

The man and I looked at each other. I would not panic. Time seemed to slow. The man leaned over me. His chest pushed out aggressively. His head thrust forward. His hands hung in loose fists at his side. *Use your head,* I told myself.

Attackers feed on their victims' fear. I would not show fear.

I forced a smile. "You made a mistake," I said confidently. "This isn't the men's room."

The man hesitated. Not much, but I saw it. His shoulders drooped. His chest sunk just a bit. He was surprised. I pushed past him, talking all the while. "I'll show you where the men's room is. Come on." I kept my voice bright, like a schoolteacher talking to a lost child. "Right through here."

I threw open the bathroom door and bolted. Without looking back I ran straight to my desk. Other employees spun around in surprise. "There's a man in the ladies' room!" I shouted. A group ran to check the hallway. I dialed building security. "There's an intruder on the third floor. Please hurry!"

Minutes later I was giving a description of the man to a policeman. "We know who he is. You were very lucky," the officer said. "We'll catch him."

Yes, I'd been lucky. I'd also been forewarned. My dream had put me on my guard.

I left work early and went home for some much-needed rest. I crawled into bed and remembered how Daddy used to make the sign of the cross over me, trusting God to protect me when he couldn't. God had protected me. He'd also reminded me I could help protect myself if I used my head, just like Daddy always said.

I turned off the light and settled down to sleep. To sleep and to dream pretty dreams.

Who Would Watch Out for Us?

Linda Roth

I shushed the kids. Driving in this snow was nerve-racking enough. I was emotionally drained that Christmas. It was the first since Jim, my husband, passed away, and I wondered how I could take care of our kids. Even this simple trip to the grocery meant that the three of them—seventeen-year-old CJ, eleven-year-old Sandie and three-year-old Ronnie—had to come with me. Now, returning home, I couldn't even enjoy the beauty of our snow-covered neighborhood. It just meant shoveling the driveway, salting the front steps, things Jim used to do. Now who would watch out for us?

Better back into the driveway, I thought as I pulled up to the house. It would be easier to unload the groceries and less difficult getting out in the morning. I backed in and put the car in park. "Okay, you kids get out of the cold and go inside. I'll bring in the groceries," I said. I watched till the kids were inside, and then opened the door and took a step out. I nearly fell on the icy driveway.

That's all I need. Better back up a little closer to the house, I thought. The less distance I had to carry the groceries, the better. I got back in, put the car in reverse and pressed down on the gas pedal. The car didn't budge. The wheels just spun. I shifted gears, tried to pull the car forward and then back, rocking it like I'd seen Jim do so many times. Still stuck.

Great. Did my car have to give me problems too? Weren't things difficult enough? Exasperated, I got out.

That's when Sandie stood up from directly behind the car. "Hi, Mom! I'm helping you get unstuck!" she exclaimed innocently. "I've been pushing."

"Never do that, Sandie!" I scolded, heart racing. *Dear Lord, what if…?* I made sure she was safely inside the house before giving it one more try. Again I put the car in reverse. This time, without hesitation, it backed up.

Who would watch out for us? I knew the answer.

No Normal Rabbit

Julie Rae Pennertz

It was one of those dreadful nights we get here in Minnesota in the middle of winter. The moisture in the air gets trapped and a curtain of fog descends all around, mixing with the snow on the ground and the flurries falling from the sky to white out everything. Normally I wouldn't drive in that kind of weather, but I'd been at a Tupperware party all evening, I was eight months pregnant and I was so exhausted I just wanted to get home already.

I was only on the road for a minute before I regretted my decision not to stay put. The winding country road was totally deserted. My car's headlights couldn't penetrate the heavy fog and the snow was getting heavier. A lot heavier. Everything beyond a few feet in front of me was a mystery. I drove slowly. I wasn't quite sure where I was, though I knew the highway should be coming up pretty soon. Shivering, I cranked up the heat. The loud blowers did their work, cocooning me from the bitter cold outside. I prayed insistently for guidance.

All at once, a small animal darted out in front of me, just within the farthest arc of my headlights. I hit the brakes and came to a skidding stop.

It was a rabbit. A snowshoe rabbit, with frosty white fur and amber eyes. I inched the car forward, but the rabbit would not get out of the way. Instead, he darted back and forth about three feet in front of my car. I tapped the horn. Instead of hopping away like a rabbit would, he sat still and stared at me, his whiskered nose twitching. He was not going to let me pass. *Come on, you silly rabbit, move!* I thought a little impatiently.

At that moment the fog ahead swirled and lifted. A bright white light seemed to come from out of nowhere. The ground shook. A massive freight train roared by just a short distance beyond the stubborn sitting rabbit. Then, with one last twitch of his nose, the rabbit darted off out of sight.

On these country roads, rail crossings have no gates, no flashing lights. No way for a tired driver on a foggy winter's night to be warned of a speeding oncoming train. Except for a rabbit that behaved the way no normal rabbit ever would.

· 10 ·

Matching Up

"May the Lord watch between you
and me. . . ."
—*Genesis 31:49*

*Open our eyes, so we can see that you want to connect
us with the people, places and things that will help us
grow spiritually and further your kingdom.*

*B*EST FRIENDS FOREVER

Judy Loggia

*M*y ten-year-old, Donna, burst through the front door. "Mom, I made a new friend at school today," she said. "Can she come over tomorrow?" Donna was a shy kid and I had been praying for her to make some friends to bring her out of her shell.

"Sure, honey, that sounds great," I said, thinking back to my own best friend growing up.

Lillian and I lived across the street from each other in Washington Heights, New York. We met at age ten too, and were instantly joined at the hip. Like my daughter, I was introverted, but Lillian drew me out and boosted my confidence. She was one of the friendliest people in school. And beautiful too—with shiny black hair, so shiny it was almost indigo, and a mile-wide smile. I knew we would be best friends forever.

Senior year of high school, Lillian went on a trip to Florida, the first time we'd be apart for more than a few days. "I'll be back soon," she told me. But three days later I answered my door to find Lillian's sister standing there, a pall across her face. "Judy...Lillian's..." She could hardly get the words out. My best friend had drowned on vacation.

Shortly afterward, my family moved to New Jersey. Over the years I lost touch with Lillian's family. But I still thought of her often. Tears formed in my eyes whenever I did. *What I wouldn't give to feel close to her again.*

The next day Donna brought her new friend home. "Hi, Mrs. Loggia," the little girl said, skipping through the front door. She flipped her hair from her shoulders— hair so shiny and black it was almost indigo—and shot me a giant smile. "My name's Lillian."

That hair. That smile. Lillian. How wonderful—my daughter's new friend was so much like the best friend I had lost.

I was still dizzy from the similarities when Lillian's mom came by to pick her up later that afternoon. I opened the door to let her in.

"Judy!" she screamed. Before I knew it, her arms had wrapped me in a tight hug. Pretty friendly for someone I had never met!

"It's me," she said, laughing. "Lillian's sister, from Washington Heights."

Yes, my daughter's friend looked familiar all right. She was my Lillian's niece. Her namesake.

THE LAST CARD

Mary Henderson

The bell rang. Recess was over. "Okay, class, time to hand in your cards," I said. "We'll be leaving soon, so put on your coats." I was taking my second graders on a holiday visit to a nursing home a few blocks away, and they'd been making cards for the residents. But we needed to get going if we were going to stick to our schedule.

I quickly collected the cards. Folded construction paper with drawings of Christmas trees, presents and snowflakes, and messages written inside. Pretty festive what the kids came up with. Except for one card. It was carefully cut in the shape of a Christmas stocking, but there wasn't any crayon or glitter on it. No decoration at all. "What happened here?" I asked the girl who made it.

"I wrote something special inside, but I didn't get to the front," she said. "Sorry I didn't finish on time, Mrs. Henderson."

"That's okay," I told her. I stuck the card at the bottom of the pile. Maybe there would be enough to go around without someone having to get this plain one. *Rush, rush,*

rush, I thought. *Why is everything so last minute at the holidays?*

I led my class on the brisk six-block walk to the home. The kids and the residents were delighted to see one another. Too bad we only had time for a few carols before a snowstorm headed our way. We hurried back to school, leaving the cards with the director.

She called me the next day. "Please tell your class thank you," she said. "The folks here loved having the kids visit. And the sweet cards too."

"What about the last one?" I asked. "It was rather plain . . ."

"It was the only card left when I got to the gentleman at the end of the hall," the director said.

"I'm sorry," I said.

"Don't be. He was overjoyed to get that card. He's blind. He ran his fingers around the edges and said, 'Why, it's a Christmas stocking. How wonderful!' Then he asked me to read the message inside." She paused. "You know what it said? 'I made this just for you.'"

"WHAT ABOUT THESE?"

Ila Mason

They've got to be here somewhere, I thought, rummaging in the bottom of my walk-in closet. I was packing for a two-week trip to Russia with a team of Americans, and I'd counted on taking along my beat-up but comfortable black sneakers. They were always right in view. *Where could they possibly be?*

Okay, I finally decided, *they've just disappeared*. So I dashed out to the store and bought new sneakers—black, sleek and sturdy with thick laces. They weren't my old reliables, but they'd do.

That night we took off for Moscow. We'd be visiting orphanages for a charity called Children's HopeChest, distributing medical supplies along with clothes and stuffed animals for the kids.

Two weeks flew by. At the last orphanage on our tour, in Lakinsk, we delivered the remainder of our supplies and were saying good-bye when the door flew open and a Russian social worker came in with two new arrivals: Sergei, twelve, and his brother, Andre, nine. The boys were crying and unkempt. Andre's toes were sticking out of his shoes, and Sergei's tattered canvas slip-ons were held together by string.

"Maybe I can find some shoes we've overlooked," our leader George said. He went out to check and managed to find a pair that fit Andre. But there was nothing for Sergei.

I looked down quickly at my new sneakers. "What about these?" I asked. I pulled them off and Sergei tried them on. "They fit perfectly," George marveled as the twelve-year-old walked excitedly around the room, testing them.

When I got home to California and started unpacking, I opened the closet door to put away my things. There were my scruffy old black sneakers, the ones I'd searched for high and low—now in plain sight, right where they should have been!

I stood there, tired but smiling. Worn-out sneakers wouldn't have done for Sergei. God's plan was for a perfect—and brand-new—fit.

CLOSE COMFORT

Frances A. Cota

I had only one regret about living in California—it was so far away from my mother in Minnesota. I loved my trips back home, going to garage sales and flea markets with my sisters and Mom, who could never resist a bargain. I had just returned to California from Mom's ninety-second birthday party—it had been a gorgeous Indian summer visit—when my family called. "Mom died last night. We'll have the funeral as soon as you can get back here."

Flying to Minnesota, I kept thinking to myself, *I should have lived closer to my mother. I should have spent more time with her.* The morning of Mom's funeral dawned raw and gray. I had packed just a thin black suit, though, recalling the warm weather only days ago. None of my sisters had a dark coat I could borrow. *Just as well,* I thought. *Everything seems so cold and lonely without Mom anyway.*

"Wait," my youngest sister said. "I think I have an answer for you. The Girl Scout rummage sale is going on today. Maybe you can find something there that would do the trick."

"Go shopping at a time like this?"

"Well, you know Mom—" She didn't have to finish. We both knew what our mom would have done.

Shivering in my light suit, I hurried to the sale. I searched the rack labeled "Outerwear Bargains." My hand lighted on a soft black down coat, just my size. The instant I slipped it on, I sensed a wonderful warmth enveloping me. *This is exactly what I need,* I thought, feeling strangely comforted.

At the funeral my older sister asked, "You okay?" and hugged me. She stepped back with a strange look.

"I got this at the rummage sale," I admitted. "I know I shouldn't have."

"It's not that," my sister said. "I cleaned out Mom's closets yesterday and brought everything to the Scouts. You're wearing Mom's old coat!"

No wonder I'd felt so wonderfully warm. Mom was home with God, and closer to me than ever.

CHARLIE'S PLATE

Kathleen H. Starling

*M*aybe you know the feeling. You're poking around at a garage sale or sifting through the stuff at a flea market when all of a sudden something just cries out, "Take me home!" It more than catches your fancy; it gets a hold of your heart. I know that feeling well. A little too well, according to my husband, Warren. "Kitty, you're too sentimental for your own good. If you keep bringing stuff home, we won't be able to close the door."

But that was before Charlie's plate came into our lives.

I found the plate at a flea market in Webster, Florida. It was seventy-five miles away from home but had great bargains. Warren claimed he was keeping an eye out for mower blades, but really he came along to make sure I didn't bring the whole market home with me.

It was good hunting. I found some beautiful carved figures for my living room and some antique kitchen utensils. It was getting late when I spotted a lady sitting on a blanket in the remotest corner of the market.

The items on her blanket paled in comparison to the others that day—sad castoffs even by my generous standards. But something caught my eye. A plastic plate with a child's drawing on it. It was not unlike a plate my daughter had made. This plate had a green stick figure, an uneven fence and a big yellow sun floating in the sky. In the corner, in neat adult print: From Charlie.

How could a mother ever part with this? I thought, picking up the plate and running my fingers over the words. Someone was supposed to love Charlie's plate. I settled on a price with the vendor and tucked it into my tote bag. Soon as we got home, I hand-washed the plate and put it in the cupboard.

The next week my granddaughters Kelly, Megan and Jami came to visit. I made the girls hamburgers for lunch. I reached in the cupboard for something to put them on. *Charlie's plate!*

"Today Grandma's got a very special plate for one of you to use," I said, holding up my latest flea market find. "It looks like something you guys might have drawn. The little boy who drew it was named Charlie."

"Grandma, what does Charlie look like?" Jami wanted to know.

"How old is he?" Megan asked.

"And why didn't Charlie's mommy want to keep the plate?" Kelly asked.

"I don't know, girls, but we can make it our very own special plate," I said. "Who wants to eat from Charlie's plate?" All their little hands shot straight up.

Charlie's plastic plate was like fine china for the girls, and for the other seven grandchildren who came along later. Everyone wanted the privilege of using it. They were quick to learn the rules. Don't put Charlie's plate in the microwave. Never use a knife on it. Wash it by hand, not in the dishwasher.

We would talk about Charlie all the time. We decided Charlie was pretty smart and a good artist. "He even made the fence smaller, so it looks like it's off in the distance."

I wondered about Charlie. Was he as cherished as his plate? Sometimes I'd find myself thinking, *Lord, wherever Charlie is, please look after him. Love him and protect him.* I knew what Warren would say. I was getting way too sentimental. But that's the way I am. I get real attached.

One Saturday maybe ten years after I bought Charlie's plate, Warren and I decided to have a garage sale. Okay, he decided. Even I had to agree that it was time to let go of a few items. We put up signs around the neighborhood, then lined up toys and furniture and clothes the kids and even the grandkids had outgrown.

That afternoon, a couple wandered up our long drive. Warren immediately recognized the man.

"Kitty, this is Roger Dillard," he said. "He has an auto repair shop down the road in Saint Cloud. I used to get our old car fixed there, remember?" Roger introduced us to his wife, Carol.

Our house is on a lake, so we started talking about fishing.

"I guess you two must go fishing a lot," Carol said.

"Not me," I said. "I can't sit still long enough. But I like finding things around the lake. Come on, I'll show you." I took Carol around to our back porch and showed her the fishing lures I had gathered over the years.

"That's a great collection," Carol said. "I'll have to tell our son about it. He's sick and homebound." Her words just hung in the air. I didn't know what to say. "I tell him stories about the people I meet, the people he can't get to see," she said, breaking the tension. Carol's eyes welled with tears. "I'm sorry. I don't know why I'm burdening you with all this. It's just that Charlie's been sick ever since he was three. Now he's eighteen, and the doctors don't give him much longer. Charlie's so sweet. He's always telling me he wishes he could do something for me."

I really wished I could do something for Carol too.

We walked back to the sale in the front yard. Roger put his arm around Carol. "I guess we should be going now," he said. I watched them head down the drive.

"Wait," I called out. "I have something for you." I dashed inside the house, grabbed Charlie's plate from the cupboard and rushed back out.

"I want you to have this, Carol," I said. I thrust the plate in her hands. "I know your Charlie didn't make this for you, but I have the feeling he would have if he could. Please take it."

Carol stared at the plate. The strangest look came over her face. Without saying a word, she turned away and hurried off. I felt terrible about upsetting her more.

Later that evening the phone rang. It was Carol.

"I'm sorry I left so abruptly, Kitty," Carol said. "I guess I was in shock. I recognized my own handwriting. This really is my Charlie's plate."

Fifteen years earlier, she told me, the day Charlie was diagnosed with a brain tumor, a nurse came into his hospital room and gave him markers and papers to draw. The hospital was going to use the pictures for fund-raisers for the children's ward. Charlie was so sick he could only do one drawing—a sunny scene, him standing by a fence. Carol jotted his name in the corner. That was the last time she saw the picture. She never knew it'd been transferred onto a plate.

"All these years the Lord looked after Charlie's plate," Carol said. "Just like he's looked after my Charlie."

Maybe the reason I love flea markets is not so much for the finds—it's for the stories. Each item I take home—whether it's an elegant figurine for my living room, antique utensils for my kitchen or a plate for my grandchildren—has its own story for me to discover. A story beyond what can be imagined.

THE KEY TO
THE STATION

Shirlee Evans

$\mathcal{E}$arly one July morning I arrived by train in Salt Lake City eagerly anticipating a week's camping trip with my son, Dan. We planned to explore the Oregon Trail. My great-great-grandfather had trudged west along that trail beside a covered wagon. Dan wouldn't arrive for a while, so I stowed my gear in a station locker and walked into town. When I returned, the station doors were locked. A sign announced it wouldn't reopen until ten o'clock that night. I peered in the window, but no one was inside.

We'd lose a whole day if I couldn't get my gear! "Lord, you've got to do something!" I demanded. I'd surprised myself. Never before had I issued an order to the Almighty.

Just then a car pulled up. A man in a suit and tie got out, jingling his keys. "Sir!" I called. I explained my problem, but he couldn't imagine how he could help. "I'm sorry the station is closed myself," he said. I noticed his full key ring. "Maybe one of those would work," I suggested.

He tried one key after the other. The last one worked! I retrieved my things, and the man locked up. "Don't understand it," he said, getting back into his car. But I understood perfectly. The Lord hadn't been put off by my presumptuous prayer. He'd sent a helpful stranger with a key that did the trick.

THE FIND BENEATH THE GRIME

Raymond L. Miller

I was a grown man when my grandmother Amanda Miller died, but it felt like I had lost a parent. That's how close we were, especially when I was little. "Ray," she used to say as we toasted marshmallows on long silver forks over her old cookstove, "you are the apple of my eye!" In our big, unruly family Gramma made me feel special and loved.

For a good while I felt a sadness I just couldn't shake, as if her love had died with her. *You should be able to get over this,* I chided myself. It wasn't like me, dwelling on the past, all the hours I'd spent with Gramma while she read me stories from the Bible. Gramma had taught me about faith, yet that too seemed to be fading.

One day my wife, Verone, and I went to a lumber-yard a ways outside town for some molding. On the drive back I realized I'd forgotten finishing nails. We were headed for the nearest town to find a hardware store when Verone spotted a yard sale. I don't much like all that musty stuff, but for some reason I stopped. While we were poking around I came across a set of grimy old forks—long-handled silver ones. *We'll use these to roast marshmallows with the kids,* I thought. *Just like I did with Gramma.*

That night as I washed the forks, my heart felt lighter, and I thanked the Lord for bringing me a bit of comfort. When I rubbed away the grime, though, I knew they were more than just a couple of yard-sale finds. There on the handles, under years of tarnish, were the initials *A.M.*—Amanda Miller. These were my Gramma's forks.

PERFECT NAME

Pauline Armstead Corson

"Mom, do you think it would be okay if I asked God for an Irish setter?" my eleven-year-old son, Brad, asked. "I already know his name."

We couldn't afford to buy a dog. Still, I answered slowly, "Yes, it is okay to ask God for a dog," wondering if I was doing the right thing.

For the next three days Brad acted as if the dog's arrival were imminent. I kept praying, *God, please don't let Brad be disappointed.*

I checked newspaper ads, asked friends and called the veterinarian to see if there were any Irish setters up for adoption. No luck. Heartsick, I told Brad the bad news.

"Don't worry, Mom," Brad said. "I know God will find one for me."

That Saturday we went to visit Brad's grandparents, who lived about seventy miles away. As we pulled up to the house I heard Brad and his brother, Scott, scream in delight. A beautiful Irish setter bounded toward us, jumping and yipping.

"My dog, Mom! He's my dog," Brad exclaimed as he and the setter romped on the lawn.

"He showed up three days ago," Brad's grandfather explained. "We chased him off, but he kept coming back." They had put an ad in the paper, but no one had claimed the dog.

"Can't we keep him, Mom?" Brad pleaded as he stroked the dog's shiny red coat. "Please . . ."

Against my better judgment I told Brad we could take the dog—for now. "But if his owners call, we need to bring him back," I warned. "So don't get attached."

Ignoring my advice, Brad said, "I know exactly what I'm going to name him—Pat."

Now it will be even harder for him to give the dog back, I worried.

The next night we got a call from the owner of the Irish setter. She explained that the dog had recently begun chasing school buses and running off. "Maybe he needs to be with children," she said. She asked about our family. I confessed that the dog seemed to be an answer to my son's prayer. "I think it's best for you to keep him," she decided.

I couldn't believe it. Then she told me about the dog's habits, the kind of food he liked—and something that convinced me Brad's plan had been God's plan all along.

"By the way," she said, "his name is Pat."

FAMILY CONNECTIONS

Natalie Garibian

$\mathcal{I}$ was a college junior on my year abroad in Paris. It should have been wonderful. It wasn't. Everything was so different: the clothes, the food, the language. I longed for something—anything—familiar. My tight-knit Armenian family was in Florida, thousands of miles away.

One Sunday I called to say hi. Their voices on the telephone were the first familiar sounds I'd heard in weeks. I cried after I hung up. I'd never felt so homesick before. *If only I were close to someone here,* I thought.

I took a walk across town. I'd passed the Armenian church in Paris many times before, but had never gone in. I realized that back in America, my family would be going to church too. Maybe being there now would make me feel closer to them.

I took a seat in the back pew just as the service started. I looked around. The priest, the prayers, the faces in the congregation—this church was a lot like my family's church in Florida. *For now, these people will be my family. Please, God, let me feel that.*

I looked up and saw an old woman coming slowly up the aisle, leaning heavily on a cane. I asked her—in Armenian—if she wanted to sit. She nodded and I slid over.

The old woman bowed her head, losing herself in prayer. I tried to pay attention to the service, but I couldn't keep my eyes off her. There was something familiar in her face; she could have been my own grandmother. But I didn't know this woman. She noticed me staring and smiled.

"You're not from here, are you?" she whispered.

"No," I said. "I come from the United States."

She nodded. After a moment, she said, "I've lost touch with them, but I used to have some nephews in America—in Florida. Sarkis, Dikran and..."

A lump rose in my throat. I knew exactly what she was going to say.

"Ara," I finished. "Ara Garibian. My father."

The old woman took my hand. *"Asdudzo kordz,"* she whispered—God's work. "I am your great-aunt. We are family."

$\mathcal{A}$MELIA'S GIFT

Lori A. Kennedy

$\mathcal{P}$layground duty wasn't a duty at all, as far I was concerned. It was one of my favorite things about teaching at Morningside Elementary School in Garden Grove near Los Angeles. I loved being outdoors with the kids and welcoming the neighborhood dogs that wandered by. Dogs often helped shy children open up and make friends.

One day I thought I'd discovered the shyest child of all. She was new at the school. At recess she leaned against the building and sucked her finger. "Her name is Amelia," a fellow teacher told me. She'd recently come from Mexico and was struggling with her English. Amelia was exactly the kind of child that made me proud to be a teacher. I believed it was my job to show her all the wonderful things she was capable of. To open her eyes to the world's endless possibilities. *I want very much to encourage her,* I prayed in the schoolyard. *Please, God, help me do my job.*

Amelia watched kids give me a hug or take my hand, but whenever I looked her way she turned her head. I made a point of smiling at her. Every day Amelia stood by the wall, communicating only with her dark brown eyes. Then one morning when I knelt down to ruffle the fur of a big black Lab, I felt a small presence beside me. "Hello, Amelia," I said. She reached for my hand. After that she no longer stood by the wall at recess.

Amelia's self-confidence increased. Soon she was playing with the other children. "Lord, we've done it!" I exclaimed the day I watched Amelia tag another child and shout, "You're it!"

All too quickly it was the last day of school. Amelia came up to me on the playground, one hand behind her back. "A surprise," she said, swinging her arm from behind her. Clutched in her hand was a small glass dog. "For you," she said, "because you love animals, and the children." The glass dog was glistening in the sun when I took it from her. "What a precious gift," I said. Amelia smiled, hugged me and ran off to play. I looked more closely at the dog and saw a chip on its right ear. Somehow that made it even more precious. *It's one of a kind,* I thought, *like Amelia.*

That fall I transferred to another school. I never saw Amelia again, but her gift had a singular place in my heart. It helped me remember the happy little girl who had once been so shy and the part I played in her transformation. I had made a difference in that child's life, and I hoped and prayed it would be lasting.

Years later I retired from teaching, packed up everything and moved to northern California. Somehow the glass dog was lost. I figured it had been left in one of the boxes I threw away. I had nothing left but a memory. *Just like my teaching life,* I thought on my blue days. *All in the past.* Not a day went by that I didn't miss it just a little.

Instead I spent much of my time learning. I often went to lectures in nearby Sacramento. One afternoon I was early for a talk, and I stopped in an antique shop to kill some time. There was a display of glass animals, and I thought about the glass dog. I asked the shopkeeper if she had ever seen one.

"They used to be popular carnival prizes," she said. "I think there's a dog in the storeroom. Let me check." A few minutes later she offered me a glass dog like the one I had lost. *Oh, Amelia,* I thought. I wondered if any of my former students had such fond memories of me. Tears filled my eyes. I held the glass dog up to the light. There was a chip on the right ear. Only angels could have orchestrated this unlikely reunion. This was the very one. This was Amelia's gift!

"How much is it?" I asked the shopkeeper. "Take it," she said. "It's not worth anything because of that chip." It was worth everything to me. It glistened in the light, just like Amelia's smile on that day so many years ago.

I arrived at the lecture hall and took a chair. I pulled the treasure from my purse, giddy almost. A young woman sat next to me, and we started talking. She was an elementary school teacher who'd come to the city to attend a workshop. "I found a flyer for the lecture in a bookstore," she said, "and here I am."

"What a coincidence," I said. "I used to be a teacher too." I held out the glass dog for her to see, and told her how it had come into my life.

She startled me with her reaction. The young woman was crying.

"Is everything all right?" I asked.

She reached for my hand. "I'm Amelia."

Was it possible?

"The dog came from the carnival," Amelia explained. "I accidentally dropped it on my way to school. That's how the ear got chipped."

Reflected in her dark eyes I saw the child I remembered.

"You taught me patience and love and kindness," she said. "Things that will last a lifetime. Things I try to pass on to my own students."

My life as a teacher wasn't lost in the past. Surely it lived on, in all my students, especially. What a gift to have run into her after all these years. Then again, there is no end to the wonderful possibilities God has in store for us. Here I am, holding Amelia's gift in my hands—and heart—once more.

BRAGGING RIGHTS

Arthur Morgan

Not long ago my wife, Alma, died after nearly fifty-eight years of marriage. She was my partner not only at home but also in my business, serving as listener, adviser and even an unpaid secretary at times. When I look back on the happiness we shared I realize ours was a match made in heaven. And I especially remember that day early in our marriage when I received the reassurance that she was meant for me.

Getting to know each other as newlyweds, we were sharing family photos. Alma pointed out different relatives and explained who was who: "This is my grandmother and that's my uncle . . ." She started to unroll a large group photograph. "I'll have you know I was once at the White House," she bragged.

"When?" I asked. She pointed at the date in the corner of the photo—1928—and I thought, *That was when my parents took me to Washington, DC.* "I went to the White House that year too," I said.

"I actually shook hands with President Coolidge," she said.

"I did too," I added. I was eleven years old at the time. I would never forget that.

"We had our picture taken in front of the White House," she said.

"So did we."

"Here I am," she said. My eyes followed her finger to a willowy schoolgirl. Then to my amazement I spotted the familiar face of a pudgy fifth grader. I drew my finger beside Alma's and said, "Here I am, right next to you." Joined in the photo before we had ever met, we were now married—and remained so for fifty-eight picture-perfect years.

"I Haven't Found the Right Thing"

Barbara Wilson

I surveyed my new kitchen. The remodeling was finally finished, but not the decorating. Thirty-five feet of countertop sat there almost empty. I'd easily filled nine feet in the old kitchen with a set of pink canisters that matched the curtains I'd put up. Now I dreamed of a blue-and-white theme. But we were out of money. It would have to wait.

Whenever someone came over to visit, we'd sit at the table for a cup of tea and chat. "When are you going to decorate this place?" they asked almost every time.

"One of these days, maybe," I'd say. "I have a blue-and-white theme in mind, but haven't found the right thing just yet." To myself I'd say, *If only I could afford it.*

One day I went into my big walk-in closet, where I like to pray, and knelt. "God, I'm sorry to bother you," I said. "I don't even know if you care about something this small, but I need help finishing my kitchen. I need something that's just right for me."

Come May, I felt especially embarrassed. I had a full house—my mom and stepdad, seven siblings and their families, grandparents and assorted aunts and uncles—to celebrate Mother's Day and my birthday, which was a few days later. The counters were still empty.

I'd just opened the card from my sisters, which had a little money in it, when the phone rang. It was a friend. "I'm at a garage sale and I found the perfect blue-and-white dishes for you for next to nothing." I couldn't leave the party, so she asked the woman who was selling the dishes to hold them.

Monday evening, armed with my birthday money, I went to see the dishes. They were perfect in every way—color, sizes, everything. If I'd had any doubts, they vanished when I flipped over one of the platters and looked at the back.

"The kitchen looks great," a neighbor said the next day. "I love the plates!"

"They were meant for me."

"Why do you say that?" she asked.

I flipped the platter over and showed her. Glazed there was a name, my name: Barbara Wilson.

· 11 ·

*C*HANGING *P*ERSPECTIVE

LEAD ME IN YOUR TRUTH AND TEACH ME. . . .
—*Psalm 25:5*

*Lord, draw us closer to you. Teach us your
ways that lead to peace and joy.*

EMPTY PEW?

Ida M. Saenz

 y five-year-old daughter, Teresa, came into my bedroom Sunday morning. "Mommy, are you going to church with me and Daddy?"

I groaned. I'd woken up with every muscle and joint aching—another flare-up of my rheumatoid arthritis. I didn't want to get out of bed, let alone go to church. "Oh, sweetie, I don't feel well."

"Church might make you feel better," Teresa coaxed. "I'll pray for you and maybe God will heal you like the leopard!" I knew she was remembering a Sunday school lesson about the leper. "Okay, I'll come," I sighed, wishing I *could* be healed.

My husband, Joe, insisted we sit up near the front. He and Teresa got into the service. But I couldn't focus on anything except the pain gripping me.

Midway through, a couple slid into the pew directly in front of us. I'd never seen them before. I would have remembered the woman's striking blonde hair. Visitors, I figured. "Welcome," I said during the greeting, leaning over the pew. "Are you new to the area?"

The blonde gazed into my eyes. "We're here to visit a friend," she said. "She's having a hard time. We want her to know everything is going to be all right." At that exact instant an enormous sense of peace settled over me. I felt healed. Not in my body—the pain was still there—but in my spirit.

I looked for the woman and her husband as soon as the service ended, but they were gone. I asked our pastor if he'd seen the couple. He looked at me, puzzled. "She'd be hard to miss with that blonde hair," I prompted.

"But, Ida, that pew was empty," he said. "No one was there." I knew better. Someone had been sitting there. Someone healing.

Everything's Falling Apart

Kevin Glaesman

I wear a size 8EEE. I always have trouble finding shoes that fit. So when I was asked to lead a wilderness trip in Yellowstone National Park I hunted high and low for a pair of good hiking boots.

I would be leading a group of young men who had histories of drug and alcohol abuse and trouble with the law. I was their counselor, a job I thought I'd be good at because I'd been there myself. For years I was an addict, in and out of jails and institutions. When I was twenty-eight, a man who'd gotten off the streets took me under his wing and helped me find a new life. Now I wanted to help others find their own miracles.

But on the trip, the boys didn't get along, and my new boots gave me blisters. One afternoon the sole of my left boot started peeling off. We had nothing with which to repair it, and the next day it simply fell apart. Everything about the trip was falling apart. *Who am I to try to help these boys?* I wondered. *I can't even pick a decent hiking boot.*

All of a sudden I felt like my sobriety was not a miracle but a fluke. Sooner or later I'd end up on skid row, where I belonged. My new life would fall to pieces, just like my boot. I couldn't help but think, *Is this how things will always be for me, Lord? Do you even care?*

Then there was a commotion among the group. "Look what I found in the bushes!" one boy yelled, running over to me. He was holding a weather-beaten boot. A left one, in wearable condition. Size 8EEE.

It fit perfectly, just like the miracle of a new life that I'd been given.

CHANGE OF HEART

Celin Wood

Birds of a feather, that was my dad and me. We loved birds, all kinds of birds, and traded notes on our sightings. He and Mom had even more feeders in their yard than I did. Dad used to make much of the fact that he'd never seen evening grosbeaks at my feeders. Large birds, easy to spot—the male with his bright yellow and black feathers, the less colorful female never far from his side. Evening grosbeaks were unpredictable migrants, but every winter flocks of them devoured the sunflower seeds in Dad's feeders just miles from where I lived. He was right. I'd never seen any in my yard. "I'll bring you some of my magic seeds," Dad said once. "Maybe the grosbeaks will surprise you one of these days." Mom laughed. "Now if they ever do come," she said, "your father will take all the credit!"

Last December Dad was very much on my mind. I'd planned a family get-together at my house for the holidays, but Dad wouldn't be there. He'd died the year before. Mom had found a new companion, a childhood friend and a widower as lonely as she was. She was obviously happy, and I was happy for her. But I struggled with accepting it. Wasn't it too soon to find another partner in life?

My holiday preparations included the birds, of course. Winter can be a hard time for them, so I filled the feeders to overflowing and clipped on extra suet cakes. The day before our celebration, I made napkin rings and place cards. I felt uneasy as I went around the table putting the cards by the dinner plates. Especially when I put someone else's at Dad's usual chair. How would he feel about that? I wished I knew. "God, help me accept this. For Mom's sake, at least."

I walked through the family room for a last-minute check. Something caught my eye at the window. A bright yellow and black bird perched on the feeder. Too big to be a goldfinch. I didn't want to move, afraid I would scare him off. But he wasn't bothered. He seemed to be trying to get my attention. Then I knew. An evening grosbeak! After all this time.

He glanced over his shoulder. *Now he'll fly away*, I thought. But I saw what he was looking at. A female sat in our lilac bush. She flew to the feeder and perched beside her partner. They stayed there, just looking at me, as if trying to make a point. "Eighteen years I've lived here," I told them, "and finally you've come. In a pair, no less. I'd love to tell my dad!" Unless, maybe, he already knew.

"Yes, Dad," I whispered. "This is quite a surprise." And, I supposed, the timing of my visit from the grosbeaks couldn't have been more appropriate. Someone else would be in Dad's chair this holiday, but I got the distinct feeling it was okay with him. We're meant to be in pairs. Mom understood. Wouldn't she laugh when she heard why I understood that now too?

WHERE AM I?

Byard Parks

I was part of a missionary group that traveled to Craiova, Romania, after the fall of communism. One thing I relished was my morning prayer time. I found an out-of-the-way overgrown cemetery, the perfect place for meditation. I memorized the path: Turn right at the yellow fence, go up the hill toward the smell of baking bread, turn left at the rose garden, pass the two barking German shepherds and then cross the sidewalk stained with mulberries.

One morning, though, I wasn't able to find the usual landmarks. "Where am I? I don't get lost this easy!" I said aloud. Finally I knelt down on the street next to the curb, bowed my head and had my morning prayers right there. Then I headed back to our lodging. The next day I had no trouble finding my way to my usual spot.

About a week later, following Bible study, two local women, Alice and Camellia, approached Dafina, a local pastor. I was perplexed when I saw them making gestures toward me.

"What were they talking about?" I asked Dafina later.

Camellia had been struggling with her faith, he explained. Early one morning something awakened her and told her to look out the window. "She saw you kneeling in the street. She was so moved that she ran downstairs to tell you she was committing her life to God, but you had left," Dafina said.

All along I thought I was lost. But someone else was lost and I was right where God wanted me.

DON'T CRY

Elise Seyfried

My Grandma Rose had Alzheimer's disease. As she grew worse, she required live-in nursing care. It was heartbreaking. She always asked the same questions over and over, like what day it was or whether or not she'd had her breakfast. We'd repeat our answers again and again. Grandma Rose never failed to ask about her grandkids. I was amazed at how Mom and my uncles repeated the same answers without ever getting impatient. They understood that despite her deteriorating mind, Grandma Rose loved her grandchildren and wanted to stay close to us.

Then, tragedy struck. My sister Maureen died in a car accident. She was only twenty-three. We were devastated. Mom especially. The day of the funeral, the whole family gathered—except Grandma Rose. After much deliberation, our family decided it would be best not to frighten Grandma with the terrible news. She wouldn't be able to retain it anyway, and the idea of repeating it was unbearable. Everyone swore not to say a word. But Mom struggled with her decision. She planned to visit Grandma

Rose soon—and dreaded the familiar litany of questions. "What will I say when she asks about Maureen?" Mom asked me. I didn't know what to tell her.

The afternoon after Mom visited Grandma, she called me. There was a long pause, then she said, "It's a miracle." When she'd visited Grandma, she'd struggled to keep a happy face and pretend everything was fine. But sure enough, Grandma wanted to know how everyone was. "How's Elise?" Grandma asked.

"She's married to Steve," my mom said. "They live near Philadelphia."

"And Carolyn?"

"Doing well, Mom. Still living in Atlanta."

Mom began to tear up, bracing herself for Grandma's next question. But instead, Grandma Rose paused. Then, with a strong voice, more alert than she'd been in years, she said, "Dear, Maureen needs you to stop crying. She's in a happier place now, except that she's worried about all of you. Maureen loves you so much. Please let her go."

HOLDING HANDS

Cathy Henn

It's a tradition in my parish to hold a special Mass every December. We have a service in a barn to commemorate the birth of Baby Jesus in a stable. It is one of my favorite events of the holiday season, and I try never to miss it.

But last year I got to the barn late. The place was packed. Priest, congregation, choir, even animals—the barn was so full that many people were standing just so they could catch a glimpse of the makeshift altar. I looked for a seat but there was none to be found. Folks were even sitting on hay bales. So when I spotted an empty picnic table under the overhanging roof outside the barn, I made my way there. I couldn't see the service inside, but at least I could hear what was going on inside.

Until we got to the part where we said the Lord's Prayer. We always do that while holding hands with the people who are next to us. Then we offer one another the greeting of peace. But sitting where I was outside the barn, I had no neighbors.

I didn't know what else to do, so I closed my eyes and held my hands out to my sides, palms up.

I felt something in my left hand. I opened my eyes and was surprised to find myself looking at a white dog. He had his paw on my palm. Smiling, I closed my eyes again and continued with the prayer, the dog keeping his paw in my hand throughout. After the amen, I heard a murmur spread through the congregation as everyone shook hands and wished one another peace. The dog seemed to cock his head as he looked at me. So I shook his paw and said to my new friend, "Peace be with you." Only then did he turn and scamper away.

Neighbors come in many forms. Especially in God's house, even if it is an old barn. I'll be sure to remember that this Christmas.

BETTER THINGS

Lisa Coburn

Cigarette smoke hung in the air around me. The club door opened, letting in a breeze from the street. A customer stepped inside. Just another man in a dark suit and tie. Traveling on business, no doubt. Graying hair at his temples gave him a distinguished air, but surely he was the same as all the rest.

I leaned against the wall, avoiding the dirty mirror inches away. I didn't like to see myself dressed as an exotic dancer. Around the club men sipped overpriced drinks, chatted up the girls, applauded the dancer onstage. I felt cold, familiar anger inside me—men were all the same. Any one of them would take advantage of me if he could. I'd learned that the hard way.

At seventeen, I'd accepted a ride home from college with an acquaintance. The drive turned into a nightmare when he forced himself on me. "Don't even think about telling anyone," he threatened. "I'll kill your family."

I didn't tell a soul. Not even my closest friends. I tried to go on with my life, but I felt like a fake. I looked like any normal student on the outside, but inside I felt dirty and worthless.

I dropped out of school. Friends and family were confused by my decision, so it seemed more important than ever to pretend I was the girl I always was. I dated a nice guy named Danny and thought I'd found my salvation when he proposed. I vowed to be the perfect wife. That would take away my shame.

But marriage didn't change a thing. How long could I keep up this charade? I was only pretending to be a respectable wife. If my husband knew the truth about me, he would leave me in a heartbeat. So I left him first.

A few months after Danny and I separated, I ran into an old classmate. "You won't believe what I'm doing," she said. "Exotic dancing at a gentlemen's club."

"How can you stand it?" I asked.

My friend shrugged. "It's no big deal. I dance in a skimpy outfit and flirt. The pay's not bad either," she said.

A place like that is where you belong, I told myself. *It's all you're good for.*

And there I was. Working in a club, hating myself as much as the men there. I kept my job a secret from Danny. One more dirty secret to add to the list.

The new customer sat down at a table. I adjusted my spaghetti straps and walked over to him. "Join you for a drink?" I asked mechanically.

"Sure," he said. "My name's James." James surprised me by ordering two plain sodas from the bar.

"So, what brings you to West Virginia?" I asked, not caring.

"I'm on assignment." I waited, but he didn't say any more. Instead he asked about me, what I wanted out of life. He talked as if I were a respectable person—which only made me more aware of my revealing costume. *Can't he see what I am?* I wondered.

"I'm due backstage," I said, getting up from my chair.

James stood up too and looked into my eyes. "Young lady," he said, "you were created for better things. God loves you. He can turn your life into something beautiful even now."

It seemed as if this man knew my secret, knew what had happened to me. But how could he? "I have to go..." I mumbled, completely shaken.

Backstage I thought about what James had said. Could things really be different for me? By the time I went back to James's table he was gone. The girls, the bouncers and bartenders, nobody remembered seeing the distinguished-looking customer.

After that encounter, I could no longer stomach my job. I quit the club and reenrolled at school. I'd have that better life. But this time it wouldn't be pretend. That meant I had to be honest—with myself and the people who cared about me. I would start with Danny. He deserved to know the truth.

Danny seemed skeptical as I settled into a chair across from him at his place. I took a deep breath. "There are things I should have told you before now. . . ."

Somehow I got it all out.

Danny looked hurt. But I could see he was hurting for me. "Now I understand why you couldn't give our relationship a fair chance," he said gently.

Danny wanted to try again. We got back together. Or maybe I should say that for the first time we truly got together. I'd tried so hard to hide. But James showed me I didn't have to go to all that trouble. God knew my secrets and still loved me. Once I felt secure in his love, I accepted my husband's love too. And finally, after so long, I began to love myself again. I wonder if that wasn't the real assignment that brought James to West Virginia.

THE ART OF LOVING

Sandy McPherson Carrubba

One afternoon, soon after I graduated from college, I walked to our city's art gallery to think about my future. I had always believed God created each of us with special gifts to serve him. My degree was in education. Did that mean I should work with children as a missionary in a far-off country? Perhaps I wasn't adventurous enough for God's work.

In the gallery I sat in front of a huge painting. A man joined me and began talking. But he was drowned out by another voice sounding in my ears: "They also serve who only stand and wait." I recognized it immediately. A line from a Milton poem. What did it mean? I must have had an odd look on my face because the man said, "I was saying I like the use of color." I got my wits about me, and the man—Joseph Carrubba—and I had a wonderful conversation. We strolled through the entire gallery together. When he asked for a date I said yes.

Joe had all sorts of ideas for his future—ideas about helping people right here at home. Now I understood what Milton's line was for. I didn't have to be a missionary to serve God. For forty years Joe and I have taught religious education to children of all ages. A lifetime together, a lifetime serving God.

BREAD AND JELLY

Cindy L. Korf

Eager to start dinner, I steered my son, Ryan, into the supermarket. An elderly woman shuffled in front of us to the shopping carts and stopped. Finally she moved off without a cart.

"Let's hurry, Ryan," I said, giving my own cart a hard push toward the bread aisle. There she was again, blocking the shelf. How had she beaten us here?

"Is this the bread on sale for fifty cents?" she asked as I reached around her.

"No, this one," I said, handing her another loaf.

She turned to Ryan. "Now I just have to find the jelly. Do you like grape jelly, young man?"

"Mom used to put it on bread for me." I remembered how we used to sit for a snack together when life wasn't so busy.

"Let's show her where the jelly is," I said. Ryan led the woman down the jelly aisle and up to the express line. "Do you have a ride home?" I asked.

"The senior bus is outside."

Ryan and I waved and moved on. Helping the woman had taken time, but suddenly it didn't matter. "Let's make sure she gets on the bus," I said, turning back. That quick the woman was gone.

"Did you happen to see an old lady with bread and jelly get on the senior bus?" I asked the cashier.

"The senior bus doesn't stop here," the cashier said. "And I haven't checked out a lady with bread and jelly."

When we got home Ryan and I talked all about the lady's mysterious disappearance—over a snack of delicious bread and jelly.

Up at Dawn

Cynthia LaShomb

Some people might think getting up at dawn to do laundry was drudgery. Well, in sultry North Central Texas that was the best time of day to be outside. I enjoyed having those early hours in the fresh air all to myself. It was my favorite time to talk to God and to listen when he talked back to me.

One especially beautiful morning I pulled my laundry out of the washing machine and headed to the yard. I pinned my clean bedsheets on the clothesline and praised God. "Your world is even more glorious than usual today, Lord," I said.

A couple of rabbits peeked out of the grass, noses twitching. Two sparrows flew overhead, chasing each other on the breeze. As they disappeared into the distance, their happy whistles were drowned out by another call, this one sad and mournful.

Hee-haw! Hee-haw!

The little donkey who lived down the lane brayed from his lonely field. I heard him most mornings, but each time it broke my heart a little. He had plenty of grass and room to roam, and the breeze was cool and comforting. Still, it made me sad to think of him all by his lonesome in the field.

"God," I said, clipping a pair of socks to the line, "I've got you to talk to. But what about that donkey over there? Who does he have to keep him company in these early morning hours?"

I made no apologies for worrying to God about an animal. From my morning talks with him, I knew that if a single one of his creatures was unhappy, God felt it. The death of a sparrow meant as much as the death of a king. God would understand my concern. "Please bless that donkey," I asked.

I picked up a towel and straightened it over the line. What was I hearing? I looked behind me and peeked around the hanging towel. The sound was strange, ethereal. Music of some sort. Or singing. Not from a radio, or like any human voice. I felt lifted up by it, as if I might float right off the ground. I stood there mesmerized, and basked in the glorious sound.

"God," I asked, "what is it?" The music faded, changed tone, and became a more familiar, discordant sound. *Hee-haw! Hee-haw!*

It was as if the beautiful, unearthly music I heard had transformed into the donkey's braying. But that was impossible. The two sounds couldn't be less alike, and I would hardly have mistaken one for the other.

Then God spoke to my heart: *What you heard was the donkey praying to me, just as he does every day. This morning I allowed you to hear how the donkey's prayers sound to my ears!*

I went back to work, the donkey's calls drifting over from his field. His braying now seemed joyous. How could any of us ever feel lonely when our God listens and speaks even to the donkey. That morning he blessed us both.

FINALLY FORGIVEN

Marie Haws

We were playing minigolf, my friend and I, but we'd gotten together that afternoon mostly to talk. Girl stuff, like clothes and guys and who was seen with whom at the movies. Definitely private conversation, and not to be shared with anyone. So when I noticed a young boy hovering behind us at the second hole, and then again at the third, I ignored him. "He's all by himself, poor kid," I said to my friend, suspecting he wanted to join our game.

Sure enough, at the fourth hole, the one with the red windmill that always blocked my ball, there he was. The boy managed a shy smile. "Will you play with me?" he asked. Leaning on my club, I looked down at him with my most adult frown. "No," I said. "Absolutely not."

The boy was crushed. I could see it in his face, almost as if I had slapped him. He dropped his club and hurried away, disappearing into the crowd.

What had I done? My friend lowered her eyes. My behavior was unforgivable, and I knew it. Only then did

I realize how much courage it must have taken for the boy to approach us, given we were so much older than he was.

For years afterward I kept wanting to call the boy back, to call the moment back and have another chance. How could I have been so selfish?

One day last summer I awoke with that memory weighing on my mind. That afternoon I even e-mailed a friend to say how much it still troubled me. "It's the one thing I can never forgive myself for," I confessed.

Coming home from the store at sundown I spotted a hand waving at me across a white picket fence. It was the woman who owned the house on the corner, out tending her rose garden. We'd chatted in passing, but with my work schedule I wasn't around much in the daytime. "Hello!" I called.

At that moment, the woman's little boy scrambled through the gate and came rushing toward me. He flung himself at me with all his strength, wrapping his arms around my legs. "Will you play with me?" he asked.

Suddenly I was back to that day years ago at the minigolf course. I looked into this neighbor boy's face and said, "Sure!" He rushed to the fence where his mother stood and grabbed a blue Frisbee. He laughed and laughed as we chased the disk up and down the sidewalk.

"Thank you for playing with me," the boy said, the twilight casting a halo around his deep-gold hair.

"I'll remember it forever," I promised. He and his mother headed inside, and I practically floated down the street toward home, the burden of that unhappy memory lifted at last.

"You're Too Young"

Chynna Laird

Ninth grade was a hard year. My mother had remarried and was now pregnant. All she could talk about was the baby. I waited alone in the cold for the city bus that took me to school. *Maybe I'm just not worth caring about,* I thought.

The bus pulled up and I took a seat. An older man in a gray felt hat got on. "Beautiful day, no?" he said, sitting down beside me. "Just enough bite in the air."

"I don't like winter much."

"Just like my granddaughter. Are you on your way to school?"

I nodded. The man took off his hat and looked at me. "You're too young to have such sadness in your heart. Focus on what makes you happy and things will work themselves out."

Normally I would have rolled my eyes at such advice, but the man looked at me as if he knew how lonely I was and he cared.

We rode together every day. Little by little I told him my story. My problems didn't seem so big now that I had a friend to talk to. And it turned out to be fun having a baby in the house. My thinking had totally turned around.

In spring my bus friend said, "Promise me you won't ever feel anything less than special." He tipped his hat and got off.

That night after dinner I sat down and wrote him a thank-you note. "You're my angel," I finished. I put the note in my book bag to give to him in the morning. But I didn't get the chance. Now that I was on the right path, he never passed my way again.

MADE NEW

Sandra Sladkey

Thanksgiving Saturday. I stared at the scene before me, a blackened wasteland that had been our home. It had been in the path of wildfires that ripped through San Diego County. Today I should have been humming carols and putting up our cherished, hand-painted Nativity scene. Now I wondered how we ever would celebrate Christmas.

I turned to the Bible for comfort after we fled the fires. The pages fell open to Isaiah: "When you walk through the fire, you will not be burned. . . . Forget the former things; do not dwell on the past. See, I am doing a new thing!"

I saw nothing new in the charred piles of rubble. A piece of corroded brass was all that was left of our daughter's bed, and those burnt springs . . . wasn't that our living room sofa? Stripped bare by the flames.

Walking through the ashes, I felt numb. What was that? A melted Christmas ornament. *Must be where the attic caved in*, I thought.

Then something else. Something white. I tugged at it. One of the shepherds from our Nativity set! I dug, my heart racing. A wise man emerged, then Joseph, an angel, Mary, the manger. Finally the Baby Jesus. The whole set, intact. Mysteriously, miraculously intact. But different. The intense heat had burned the paint off, turning the figures a beautiful, pure white. They were transformed. Made new. And in time, our home—and we—would be too. Mysteriously, miraculously renewed.